Queer at Work

Sasmita Palo • Kumar Kunal Jha

Queer at Work

palgrave
macmillan

Sasmita Palo
School of Management
and Labour Studies
Tata Institute of Social Sciences
Mumbai, India

Kumar Kunal Jha
School of Management
and Labour Studies
Tata Institute of Social Sciences
Mumbai, India

ISBN 978-981-13-8561-2   ISBN 978-981-13-8562-9 (eBook)
https://doi.org/10.1007/978-981-13-8562-9

© The Editor(s) (if applicable) and The Author(s), under exclusive licence to Springer Nature Singapore Pte Ltd. 2020
This work is subject to copyright. All rights are solely and exclusively licensed by the Publisher, whether the whole or part of the material is concerned, specifically the rights of translation, reprinting, reuse of illustrations, recitation, broadcasting, reproduction on microfilms or in any other physical way, and transmission or information storage and retrieval, electronic adaptation, computer software, or by similar or dissimilar methodology now known or hereafter developed.
The use of general descriptive names, registered names, trademarks, service marks, etc. in this publication does not imply, even in the absence of a specific statement, that such names are exempt from the relevant protective laws and regulations and therefore free for general use.
The publisher, the authors and the editors are safe to assume that the advice and information in this book are believed to be true and accurate at the date of publication. Neither the publisher nor the authors or the editors give a warranty, express or implied, with respect to the material contained herein or for any errors or omissions that may have been made. The publisher remains neutral with regard to jurisdictional claims in published maps and institutional affiliations.

Cover illustration: Thomas Howey and eStudio Calamar

This Palgrave Macmillan imprint is published by the registered company Springer Nature Singapore Pte Ltd.
The registered company address is: 152 Beach Road, #21-01/04 Gateway East, Singapore 189721, Singapore

Preface

This book is the result of five years of research, observation and interaction with the LGBTQ community from various part of India. This would have not been possible without the help and courage of all the individuals from the LGBTQ community who have opened their hearts to tell their story and are striving to bring positive change in the society. Initially, this research was conducted by as part of my MPhil and PhD research. Such is the situation of the LGBTQ individuals in India that there were more reasons that I saw for not taking up this research rather than going ahead with it. One factor that outweighed all the other factors was the fact that I wanted to explore my own identity as a queer individual. I wanted to go on a journey to know who I was as a person. This journey would not have been possible without the support of Professor Sasmita Palo who has also authored this book with me. Working with Professor Palo not only gave me clarity with regard to the apt way of moving forward with this project but also enabled us to do triangulation as we were now looking at the issues faced by the LGBTQ community from an insider as well as an outsider perspective.

The main aim of this book is to bring out the voices and experiences of individuals from the LGBTQ community in the workplace. At the same time, this book also aims to sensitise leaders, change agents, human resource and diversity managers with all the possibilities and limitations associated with diversity and inclusion of LGBTQ individuals not only in the workplace but also with regard to recognising LGBTQ rights as human rights in the society. In the initial phase of the research, we conducted 31 semi-structured in-depth interviews with individuals from the

LGBTQ community working in formal manufacturing and service sectors. The sampling was purposive in nature and we used the snowballing technique to reach individuals from the community. We have also included our observations while interacting with people and spaces during the duration of the research.

The readers will be introduced to the normative and the non-normative definitions around gender and the manner in which we perform gender. We thought that it was crucial to give an "introduction to gender" as we realised that during the research most of the individuals did not have clarity on what really gender is and if there is an "alternate" way of performing it. Our definition of gender is inclusive and we do not claim that it is the ultimate and the most apt. The intention is to clear confusions around gender by questioning the very basis on which it is constructed. We believe that questioning the basis on which gender is constructed in our society will help us not only to deconstruct the way gender is viewed but also in reconstructing new lenses of viewing gender which are more inclusive. The readers will notice that in the first few chapters they will have small caselets, where they are asked questions with regard to how they would solve a problem or react if they were in a certain situation. The caselets are drawn from the experiences of the individuals from the LGBTQ individuals in their workplace. This will give an opportunity to the readers to step into the shoes of an individual who either has a non-normative gender or sexual orientation identity or is in a position where they might have the power to address certain situation faced by an individual from the LGBTQ community. Doing this would help the readers to see the same situation from different perspectives. In the later part of the chapters, the readers will be directly exposed to verbatim from the interviews conducted with the individuals from the LGBTQ community.

While reading this book, the readers will notice that at some places, we (the authors) have shifted from "we" to "I." "I" has been used in the research to highlight the insider perspective of our co-author who identifies as queer. "We" has been used to bring out the findings and observations that both the authors have had together during the research. At some places, we have also used "LGB" instead of "LGBT." This is mainly because recent changes in the law have given legal recognition to the transgender community. Further, we have also used "LGBTQ" to signify any gender and/or sexual orientation identity that does not meet the expectations of the heteronormative society. Though we have tried our best to bring in the differences in the issues faced at the workplace by lesbian, gay, bisexual and transgender individuals, this book mostly covers what in general an individual from the community, who may or may not have disclosed their identity to their employers, faces due to their non-normative sexual orientation and gender identity.

We understand that there are many limitations of this research. Some of them are not being able to properly represent the voices of individuals who identify as asexual or intersex or covering only the formal manufacturing and service sectors which are mostly located in the cities that hardly represent eight per cent of the Indian population. Another criticism could be that we are looking at sexual orientation and gender identities in singularity and not accounting for intersectionality. We could also be criticised for the language being too simplistic for the gender discourse that most academicians emphasised upon in the past. We have tried to keep the language for this book lucid as we believe that a large part of the society should be exposed to conversations which have been considered "difficult" or "tabooed" from a very long time. We would consider ourselves grateful if we can initiate this difficult conversation on a larger level and eventually move beyond these conversations towards creating a more inclusive society for all. We would urge our readers to comment, criticise and question what we have written as we believe that it is an integral part of furthering any conversation.

Mumbai, India

Sasmita Palo
Kumar Kunal Jha

Acknowledgement

From not being sure if we will be able to take up this project to this! We have come a long way and we have not done it alone. There are a number of people for whom we are grateful. We wish to thank the entire Tata Institute of Social Sciences (TISS) community for making TISS a space where one has the freedom and courage to take up research topics that very few dare to study. A special thanks to each and every individual associated with the School of Management and Labour Studies at TISS.

This project would not have been possible if not for MD Zubaer. Thank you for not only helping us envision the creative and the idea of cover design for this book but also always providing moral support and encouragement when we hit the writer's block. We would like to thank Professor Bino Paul and Dr Tarun Menon for always being there and helping us strengthen the research methodology. We would like to thank Abhishek Tambhi without who data collection would have taken ages!

Thanking the individuals who agreed to participate in the research would not even be an iota of what they have done for us. Thank you for being brave, for trusting us, and for sharing your pain, sorry and happiness with us. All of you are our role models. Thank you.

We would like to thank our parents and all the people who encouraged us to do this research. Even though there were a few who believed in this project, it is because of their faith that we are able to write this acknowledgement. Having said this, we would also like to thank all the voices that discouraged us from taking this project—you played an important role as well!

We would like to thank everyone for supporting us at each and every step of this project from our publishing house—Palgrave Macmillan.

Contents

1 **Introduction to Gender** 1
Research Methodology 1
Introduction and Historical Context 3
Traditional Understanding of Gender 4
Conditioning and Bias 5
The Gender Quiz 6
Authentic Gender Model 6
NALSA Verdict 12
Section 377 of the Indian Penal Code (till September 2018) 18
Section 377 of the IPC After September 6, 2018 19
LGBT Community and the Workplace 21
References 30

2 **Accepted as the Other: Discrimination, Identity Crises and Coping Mechanism** 33
Non-Verbal Discrimination 34
Verbal Discrimination 37
Physical Discrimination and Sexual Harassment 40
Fear of Discrimination 43
Managing Information Related to Non-Normative Identity and Coming Out 45
Strategies to Come Out 49
The Impact of Discrimination 52
Identity Crises 54

	Living in Fear	55
	Courtesy Stigma	56
	Coping Mechanism	57
	References	62
3	**Heteronormativity in the Workplace**	63
	Heteronormativity in Organisations	66
	Married or Gay?	66
	Heteronormativity and Body Language	71
	Heteronormativity and Gender Appropriate Dressing	75
	References	80
4	**Queer, Information Technology and Internet: The Virtual and the Real**	81
	Internet Gave Me an Identity	86
	Discrimination	95
	References	103
5	**Are Indian Organisations Safe for the LGBTQ Employees?**	105
	Are Some Industries More Accepting Than Others?	111
	Can LGBTQ Employees Lead Organisations?	117
	Does Diversity and Inclusion Policy Matters?	122
	References	126
6	**Conclusion**	127
	Need to Start Somewhere	128
	Initiating Difficult Conversations	129
	Creating Safe Spaces and Giving Space to People	130
	Everyone Is Valued	131
	When It Is All About Productivity	131
	Having a Clear Stand	133
	Glossary	135
	Index	139

CHAPTER 1

Introduction to Gender

It was only just over two decades ago in 1990 that the World Health Organization removed homosexuality from its list of mental diseases. Nevertheless, over 70 countries are participating in the United Nations which still classify homosexuality as a criminal offence. Even in developed countries which have anti-discrimination law to protect individuals from the LGBT community, the hate crime that the community has to face has been one of the highest. Further, the LGBT community is subjected to non-violent discrimination, indifferent behaviour which is often not recorded. In India, discrimination, hate crime, violence and stigmatising attitudes on the LGBT community is often justified on the bases of social, religious and traditional beliefs and value system. Before we deep dive into this topic, we would briefly like to introduce our readers about the research methodology and approach while writing this book. We have explained the research methodology in detail in the preface of this book, so we will keep it short over here.

Research Methodology

This book is the result of over five years of research, observation and interaction with the LGBTQ community from various parts of India. Since we wanted to explore the issues of queer and non-normative sexual orientation and gender identities specifically at the workplace, and to record the experiences and voices of the individuals from the community at their workplace, our approach for the research has been qualitative. We started this research with semi-structured in-depth interviews in the metropolitan city of Mumbai and Hyderabad. Over the years, we have been able to be present and observe various spaces in the society that have been considered as safe spaces by some individuals from the LGBTQ community. We have also mentioned reflections on our journey while undertaking this research. At some places, the readers will see the use of the pronoun "I," while at other spaces we have used the pronoun "We." The places where the pronoun "I" has been used is an insider perspective on the LGBTQ community given by one of our co-authors. We have tried to keep the language as simple as possible, but we have not defined the meaning of terms such as gay, lesbian, queer, cis-gender and so on. During the research, we have often noticed that a few words were misunderstood, the meaning of some words was not clear to many individuals and some words were often used interchangeably due to lack of awareness by many people in the society and, at times, even by individuals who are from the community. So we have given a glossary towards the end of the book with the definition of some of these words. We advise the readers to go through these words even when they think they are aware of them. One way of making this exercise interesting is that the readers can first see the word, try to define it on their own and then see if there is any difference in their definition and the definition given in the glossary. However, we do not claim that these definitions are most apt and various factors affect the way they may be used.

Another thing that the readers will notice while reading this book is that at most of the places we have used acronym LGBT, while at other places we have used the acronym LGBTQ, LGBTQIA or LGB or queer to describe the community. There is a difference between all of them and their usage. Most of us would be aware that the acronym LGBT stands for Lesbian, Gay, Bisexual and Transgender. When we use the acronym LGBTQ, LGBTQIA or the word queer we are referring to the larger community which includes various identities such as intersex, asexual, pansexual and attempts to include minority and non-normative gender and sexual orientation identities. Similarly, when we use the acronym LGB or LBT, then we are only referring to Lesbian-Gay-Bisexual individuals and Lesbian-Bisexual-Transgender individuals respectively. The reasons for excluding "T" at some places is because there have been some changes in the legal recognition of the transgender community in India and the transgender community may have legal rights with respects to their non-normative identity which individuals from the gay, bisexual and queer community may not have. This is mainly because the NALSA verdict (National Legal Services Authority v. Union of India verdict) which legally recognised transgenders as the "third gender" was passed before the decriminalisation of Section 377 of the Indian Penal Code (IPC). We have briefly attempted to cover the NALSA verdict and Section 377 of the IPC in various chapters of this book.

The period of data collection for this book has majorly been during 2013 to 2018, a time when homosexuality was considered a criminal activity in India. We believe that this makes the research interesting and one of its kind, as it records voices of individuals from the queer community at a time where the act of even consensual same-sex activity was criminalised by the Supreme Court which ruled out the High Court verdict of decriminalisation of homosexuality in the year 2009. Since the Supreme Court had re-criminalised homosexuality in 2013, many individuals from the community who had come out or were planning to come out had to go back in the closet. In this chapter and subsequently in the book, we have also attempted to answer if a change in the law facilitates any positive change in the lives of the LGBTQ individuals.

Introduction and Historical Context

There has been an account of the existence of the queer community throughout Indian history. Today, these historical accounts are often brought in as an argument by LGBT right activists, and allies in the debate against the stereotypical believe that LGBT identities are a gift of western culture. On the contrary, in India, there have been various accounts that help us to conclude that people from the LGBT community have existed even before the British invasion. Further, people from the community have been recognised and accepted as a part of the society in the pre-British colonisation era. It was the western societies that have been responsible for suppressing sexuality. Foucault (1976) writes about the way sexuality was suppressed by the western societies from the seventeenth to mid-twentieth centuries as a result of the rise of capitalism and bourgeois society in the first volume of *History of Sexuality*. It was a result of this suppression that Section 377 of the penal code which criminalised homosexuality was introduced in the British colonies—a regressive law that existed in India till late 2018 and criminalised even consensual same sex between adults. Today, most of these western societies have been trying to rectify their mistakes and problems caused due to suppression of human sexuality. This is not only leading to higher acceptance of the LGBT community and sexual minorities but also helping the societies to be more aware and open about gender and sexuality. These societies are now moving beyond the traditional gender model, and people are relatively more open towards having conversations around a subject which was/is considered taboo for a very long time. It is not that all individuals in these societies agree with these attempts of rectification, but these societies have been able to create space for difficult conversations successfully and have recognised LGBT rights as human rights. These conversations, attempts around rectification of past mistakes undertaken predominantly by the western society, and lack of awareness and/or partial rejection of the historical development of human sexuality lead individuals/groups in India to think that recognising LGBTQ rights is a western conspiracy that intends to bestialise and infect their own culture.

One of our observations was that most individuals who identified as heterosexuals in India and, at times, even self-identifying individuals from the LGBT community did not know much about the LGBT community and their perceptions of the community were based on common stereotypes. We realised that the primary reasons for these biases, questions and curiosity that a large part of Indian society has towards the community are a result of the traditional understanding of gender model and lack of awareness on the issues of sexuality—which does include not only non-normative sexuality and gender identities but also normative ones. This is not surprising in a country where it is still debated if sex education should be part of school education curriculum. Nevertheless, we also felt that more people were open to having discussions and that it was not very difficult for us to initiate conversations which are considered to be difficult and tabooed.

Traditional Understanding of Gender

Traditional understanding of gender categorises gender into two categories of male and female depending on the biological sex of the individual, thus viewing gender in a binary. It is the biological sex of the individual that defines the boundaries of gender identity, gender role and its sexual orientation to the opposite gender. Even though India is a nation with enormous cultural diversity—gender role, gender identity and sexual orientation of the individual is based on the traditional model of gender where the role and identities of men and women have clear demarcation. Even in few matriarchal societies gender role and identities of its people, though different from patriarchy, is based on traditional gender model where biology becomes destiny. Thus, a child born with a penis would be considered male, would be expected to be self-identified and also collectively identified with/by the socially constructed identity of a man most apt to that society, expected to adhere to the cultural definition of masculinity, perform all the roles that is appropriated for a man in that particular society and have sexual orientation towards the opposite gender that is a woman. Similarly, a child born with a vagina is labelled as a female, expected to be feminine, play the role that is considered appropriate in that society and have a preference for the opposite gender that is a man. Anything that does not fit in with the above model is considered as non-normative and deviant—often resulting in the society taking or considering "corrective" measures which cause discrimination, stigma and violation of the individual's human rights. Though what is considered appropriate by the traditional gender model has evolved over a period of time, and there is an increasing overlap between the gender role and the identity of men and women—a majority of the society(ies) still has/have not been able to move beyond the binary of the traditional gender model. It is difficult to do away with these identities and concepts as a result of constant direct and indirect conditioning which begins as soon as the child is born or even before that when the gender of the foetus is determined in the mother's womb.

CONDITIONING AND BIAS

One of the instances where I realised the depth of integration of these conditionings in human nature was when I was finding it difficult to switch from a female to male pronoun for a friend whom I had known for a very long time after his coming out to me. Even after reading and being exposed to gender theories, I would address this friend in the female pronoun only to realise after I had spoken that I was using the wrong pronoun—correcting myself and again making the same mistake. I was finding it challenging to address my friend in the desired pronoun as I had known him for a very long time and had got used to addressing him with a female pronoun. I had to be really reflexive and mindful of my speech to not repeat my mistakes. Before this instance, I thought that I was very mindful and sensitive at least with gender issues. It was then I realised that it was so challenging to do away with the conditioning just because I had got used to and was comfortable with it. I could understand the reasons that it is difficult for a society to have even positive changes that lead to the inclusion and celebration of diversity as a result of conditioning which would make most members/institutions in the society uncomfortable. In fact, we are so comfortable and used to the gendered language that most would like to keep their comfort and privilege even at the cost of lives of other individuals who do not conform to the norms in the same society.

The Gender Quiz

Due to our work in the area of gender, we had opportunities to provide gender and sexual harassment training to organisations and individuals across India. During these training interventions, we decided that we will test if providing gender sensitivity training to individuals actually makes them sensitive towards concepts and issues related to gender. So we developed the gender quiz. First, we discussed the traditional gender model where the biological sex of an individual determines the gender role, gender identity and sexual orientation with our participants. While explaining the same, we would also ask our participants to list and discuss the gender bias or segregation that they have witnessed as a result of the traditional gender model that we have been living in. After this, we discussed the authentic gender model which is given by Samuel Lurie.

Authentic Gender Model

The authentic gender model, given by Samuel Lurie, gives room for inclusion of more gender expression. Authentic gender model overcomes the shortcoming of the traditional gender model which is based on a binary system of recognising biological sex as male or female, gender role as masculine or feminine, gender identity as a man or a woman, and sexual orientation towards only the opposite biological sex leaving room for recognition of only heterosexual individuals. In the authentic gender model, intersex is included as a biological gender which leads to the recognition of more than two biological sexes, thus negating the gender binary. Further, in gender roles, androgynous roles are also included. The stereotype that an individual with certain biological sex is supposed to play only the appropriate role to their sex is also broken. This model further recognises "unique" gender identity which are/might be different from the traditional gender identity that is again based on the biological sex at the birth of an individual. This model recognises that an individual may or may not identify with the traditional gender identities and thus have unique or queer gender identity/

identities. Further, this model recognises heterosexuality as not just the only sexual orientation but also sexual orientation identities such as gay, lesbian, bisexual, pansexual and asexual identities. After the introduction to authentic gender model, most of our participants felt that they would not have faced the stereotypes and our society would have been more inclusive if this would have been the outlook for our society with regard to gender rather than relying on the binary of traditional gender model. Even though most of our participants thought that the authentic gender model was better than the traditional gender model, we wanted to test if these individuals can get rid of/recognise the gender bias they still had as a result of continuous direct and indirect exposure and the expectation of confirming with the traditional gender model.

So once we had explained the authentic gender model, we gave our participants a quiz. In the first part of the quiz, the participants were shown three pictures; each picture had two individuals (models) in the frame. We did not disclose the gender or the sexual orientation of the models in the picture to the participants. All the participants assumed the first picture to be that of a man and a woman, the second picture appeared to be that of two men, and the third picture appeared to be that of two women. We told the participants that one of the three pictures is that of a couple and that the participants had to guess which picture was that of a couple in a relationship. Majority of the time the participants thought that the first picture that appeared to be that having a man and a woman standing together was the picture of a couple. This confirmed that even after discussing the flaws of a traditional gender model and discussing the authentic gender model, it was easier for the participants to choose a man and a woman (or individuals who came across as heterosexuals) as a couple in a romantic, emotional and sexual relationship as compared to that of a man with another man as well as a woman with another woman. The reason given by most of the participants for choosing the first picture was that most had not known any self-identifying person from the LGBT community personally. Some knew people from the LGBT community in India, but then they did not know anyone from the community who was involved or had discussed with them about their partners and relationship. Further, most participants also felt that given the information that one from the three pictures shown to them were a couple, they choose the picture of a man and a woman as it was more "natural" and normative for people from the opposite genders to be in a relationship, and also the probability that people from the LGBT community would come out with their partners with the prevalence of Section 377 of the IPC was relatively less.

After the participants had shared the reasons for selecting the first picture, we asked them the factors that enabled them to reach the conclusion of the gender and the sexual orientation of the individuals shown in the picture. It was after this question that most of the participants realised that they were still using the traditional gender model as their world view. Most of the times biological sex, gender identity, gender role and the sexual orientation of an individual are assumed by the way gender is performed. Further, this performance of the gender is based on the traditional gender model, if not it becomes deviance. Just from the picture or appearance, though one can guess the gender of an individual most of the time from the traditional model as there is only room for male and female in the traditional gender model, but one cannot know for sure the gender, gender identity or the sexual orientation of the individual as there is not enough information. The best way to have information related to the gender of an individual is from the individual themselves. Even this is not a full proof way of knowing for certain due to various reasons such as criminalisation by the law and stigmatisation by society. Further, it is not necessary that the gender of the person once disclosed or even when not disclosed remains constant throughout for each individual. Interestingly, disclosure of the gender is assumed to be done mostly when the individual does not identify with the normative gender binary structure or is not present to perform gender for others to assume if they fall into a non-normative gender category. The most important point to be noted is that each individual has the right to gender expression, the gender of a person should not be assumed and that gender is fluid.

After we completed the discussion around the first set of pictures for the gender quiz, we went to the next set of pictures. In the next segment of the quiz, we showed the participants three pictures just like the first time. The first picture was that of what appeared to be of a man and a woman, the second picture appeared to be that of two men, and the third picture appeared to be that of two women. The only difference between the first set of pictures and the second set of pictures was that all the (model) couples in the pictures were kissing each other. For most of the participants, the first reaction was that of surprise and at times even of shock, once the picture was exposed to them. The surprise was from the fact that most of the participants had not expected to see two people from the same gender kissing each other in a picture in a public space with many other individuals around them. Few also reported not having seen people from the same gender kiss or be in an intimate relationship before, even in a picture. From this, we could set a realisation with most of the participants that even after sensitisation it is difficult and takes time to be mindful of the body language and reactions formed instantly when the mind is exposed to what has been considered deviance from a long time.

Then we asked our participants about which picture they thought was that of a couple in a sexual, romantic as well as an emotional relationship with each other? Most of the time we would get the answer that people in all three pictures are in a relationship with each other as they are kissing each other. Sometimes a few participants would say that it could not be determined which picture was that of a couple, but they could not reason how they reached this conclusion. Then we discussed with our participants of what can be an act of cultural sanction for labelling people to be in a relationship. We then asked our participants if a closeted gay man kisses a woman or does culturally appropriate things that a heterosexual man would do in a society, will he be considered a heterosexual man or would his identity still be that of a gay man. At times, when participants were not able to understand the question, we would simplify the same by asking them if a self-identified gay man has a sexual relationship with a heterosexual woman then will the man become heterosexual. By this point, most of our participants understood that just being involved in a sexual relationship with the "other" gender will not change the identity of the individual, but gender and sexual identity are fluid, thus only the individual could determine their gender and sexual identity. This exercise helped our participants to understand that a heterosexual individual would not necessarily become homosexual just because they have been in a sexual relationship with another person from the same gender and vice versa.

During the time span of this research, we have come across many individuals who are closeted gay or lesbians, but are married to people from the "opposite" gender because of pressure to conform to the norms of the society. After a certain age, marriage becomes an important factor for most individuals to be in alignment with the heteronormative structure of society. We have covered heteronormativity in detail in our third chapter. So we cannot be sure if the people in the picture, even when they are kissing, are a couple or in a relationship.

Then we asked our participants to assume that people in all three pictures from the second set were a real-life couple, which picture was that of a straight couple or a heterosexual couple? All the participants in all the training sessions either thought that the first picture was that of two individuals who appear to be a man and woman and were kissing had to be that of the straight couple, or the audience did not have an answer. Then we asked our participants the definition of the term straight or heterosexuals, to which most of the participants generally answered that a relationship between a man and a woman or a relationship between two opposite gender would be a heterosexual relationship. After the participants had defined the relationship between heterosexual couples, we asked them how they concluded that the picture that they had chosen was that of a man and a woman. The answers were again based on assumptions, where the participants had assumed the gender of the couples in the picture based on their appearance. However, this time the assumptions had become stronger, now that the couple in the picture was seen being intimate with their partners. Soon the participants realised that they had repeated the same mistake and that it was challenging even after sensitisation and training to change the thought process unless one can be mindful about the same.

Once a participant asked an interesting question after the discussion:

If I were to ask each person about what gender identity and sexual orientation they identified before every conversation and not assume their gender then I will go crazy? This will make conversation with anyone so difficult.

A complete deconstruction of the concept of gender is not possible, but the idea is for individuals to understand and to be sensitive to different forms of gender expression and deconstruct those constructs of gender which would offend and suppress specific gender and sexual orientation identities in our society. This can be done with an attempt to understand the construction of gender in different societies or to begin within their own society/societies and themselves. Further, we need to understand that we do not need to know the gender identity and/or sexual orientation of everyone that we talk to or have an interaction with. Still, in our mind, we think that we know and that it is essential for us to know when there is uncertainty with regard to the gender and sexual orientation of individuals. Most of the time, we do not question the gender and/or sexual orientation of an individual because of the visible part of it, the way it is performed and assumption of all genders being in the normative gender category. Almost everyone in the society is assumed to be cis-gender, heterosexual falling in line with the gender identity and role that they are supposed to be as per their biological gender. So any deviance from the above is not expected, and the mind becomes alarmed/curious in a situation of uncertainties. This practice of assumption and expectations from others to perform gender in a way that there is no difficulty for others to assume and interpret the same becomes the root cause of stereotypes and rejection of non-conformance in sexual orientation and gender identities. This indirectly puts pressure on people in society to identify with the sexual orientation and gender identity that is approved by the society. Individuals have to choose and are directly and indirectly trained to choose a gender expression that is deemed to be fit in accordance with society without any deviation. Thus, it is the larger collective of individuals and society that dictates and does not allows exploring and choosing freely the sexual orientation and gender role that we want to perform. Even when individuals try to do away from the traditional gender model and not assume, it becomes extremely difficult as time, and again one is reminded to conform. Unlearning becomes key to "un-gendering" that is the process to do away with only acceptance of a certain way of confirming as a result of heteronormativity. Can the human mind be free from all gender assumptions and even if it can, will it not form new assumptions and what happens when this newly formed assumptions that are considered unbiased become normative and cause a similar problem? Any individual who is trying to do away with the traditional gender model or questions the existing structures or decides to be respectful to everyone's right to gender identity and expression have to be mindful and reflective.

At times, it becomes difficult even after being mindful to not assume, but it is the intention of the individual that matters. The intention of acknowledging, being reflective, being mindful and respecting all individuals' right to gender identity, gender role and sexual orientation would go a long way even when these assumptions are not right.

For instance, the cultural sanction of *Hijra*[1] where these expectations are set not just by the larger society but also by other individuals identifying as *Hijra* themselves. There is evidence of the existence and role of the *Hijra* community even in the pre-colonial era, but this does not mean that the *Hijra* community has the same respect and rights as the heterosexual population of the country. The primary source of livelihood for the *Hijra* community has been either begging, *badhai (blessing) and/or sex work*.[2]

---

[1] Often used under the umbrella of transgenders even when *Hijra* as an identity is not just related to gender but to also economic, career, political and socio-cultural roles that an individual identifying with this identity is allowed to perform. One *might argue that gender of any individual impacts the economic, career, political and socio-cultural status in the society*, while this is true but in case of individuals identifying with the *Hijra* identity these aspects are made more rigid to such an extent that there is no longer a choice but expectations.

[2] Or sex-work. The translation for *badhai* would be blessing or congratulations. One of the sources of income for the *Hijra* community in India has been conducting blessing rituals in functions especially functions related to the birth of a child in a family.

However, the cultural sanction has majorly remained only till the community has confined to the already predefined roles. In fact, the confinement for a large part of the community is been restricted not only by the society but at times also by their own *gharana*[3] and *guru*.[4] Thus the recognition of the *Hijra* community in the Indian society remains restricted only to the culturally defined role which has not changed from a very long time.

In fact, this culturally limited role for the *Hijra* community has been so strong that even the government bodies in South Asian regions of India and Pakistan had reinforced and failed to think beyond them while trying to help this marginalised community. Not very long ago, *Hijras* were recruited as tax collectors in some regions of India and Pakistan. As a tax collector, their role was to go at the residence of the tax defaulter and curse (which is the opposite of *badhai*), so that the defaulter would be embarrassed in their society. The *Hijras* would keep doing this every day till the tax defaulter pays the arrears to the income tax department. Here, even though the government may have recognised the need to provide sources of new livelihood to the community, they failed to address the stigma attached with being a *Hijra* as even the government thought that the best a *Hijra* could do is cause embarrassment and fear amongst the people in the society. Though this practice of employing *Hijras* as tax collectors is not in practice, even today most people fear, are embarrassed and disgusted by the community.

NALSA Verdict

On April 15, 2014, the Supreme Court granted transgenders the third gender status in our society. The court recognised that the transgender community have been kept away from the fundamental human rights since a long time and ruled that no individual should be snatched away from opportunities which are very basic to them due to their gender or sexual orientation identity. Many parts of the judgement oppose the judgement of Section 377 of IPC, though it had not ruled out the judgement of Section 377. Thus, though recognised legally, transgenders were still falling under the preview of Section 377 which criminalises consensual same-sex act in

---

[3] *Gharana* is a closed community of *Hijras*. There are various *gharana* in India, and the *Hijras* associated with a particular *gharana* have to abide by the rules of the *gharana*.

[4] The literal translation of the world *guru* is a teacher. Though *guru* is a commonly used word in Hindi, in this context *Guru* is the head of the *gharana* and is mostly the eldest *Hijra* in that *gharana*. The *Hijras* of a *gharana* have to consult and get the approval of the *guru* for any decision which falls outside the already defined rules of the *gharana*.

adults. The NALSA verdict does not make it compulsory to undergo sexual reassignment surgery to identify as a transgender individual, but then limits the gender that a transgender person can have consensual sex with by not ruling out Section 377 of the IPC, which implies that the traditional gender model which follows the binary was reinforced at all times as an individual should have sexual orientation only towards the opposite gender. Further, there has been a lot of confusion with regard to the definition of "transgender." Even though it has almost been over three years since the judgement has been passed there have not even been real attempts to implement it. Though on paper we might be moving in the right direction, the translation of this law into praxis has not been even close to addressing the problem.

Various incidences of *Hijras* being raped and assaulted by policemen have also been reported. Further, people trying to protect the community have also been detained and harassed by the police. According to the Telangana Hijra Transgender Samiti (THTS), there have been more than 30 attacks on transgenders from July 2014 to December 2014 in Telangana region alone. Of all these cases, only one FIR has been registered so far. Transgenders have reported that the police have refused to register their complaint on several instances and even when the complaint is registered, it is not thoroughly followed up. Due to this indifference from the authorities, the transgenders have stopped going to the police station to lodge complaints about such instances. These instances of violence have been recorded after the Supreme Court has recognised and given transgenders in India the status of "third gender" through the NALSA verdict. It is not surprising that even today in India the situation, condition and stigma attached with being a transgender in the society has not witnessed any real positive changes.

Many individuals from the community are now opposing the implementation of the changes in the transgender bill and are demanding the first version of the bill. The Transgender (Protection of Rights) Persons Bill of 2016 is considered problematic due to the following principal reasons:

1. This bill does not uphold the right of self-identification as a transgender which was considered as a fundamental constitutional right as stated in the Supreme Court judgement in NALSA versus Union of India verdict. As per the new bill, a mandatory physical screening by the District Screening Committees would certify if an individual "qualifies" to be a transgender person.

2. Further, this bill not only redefines who can be a transgender, but also confuses intersex individuals as transgender.
3. Even though the bill is titled "Protection of Rights" for transgender persons, it criminalises begging which is one of the primary sources of survival for most of the individuals from the *Hijra* community. The bill further upholds only the right of birth families and rejects families of choice for transgender persons. It also remains silent on affirmative action in education, employment and healthcare.

The Immigration and Refugee Board of Canada, Ottawa published a report named *Situations of Homosexuals: Availability of Support Group and State Protection* in the year 2009, where the situations of the queer community in India for the period of June 2004 to April 2009 were reported to be in a critical condition. This report studies, research and cases from 2004 to 2009 and brings to our notice that people from the queer community have often faced "queer bashing," loss of job and residence, and forcefully detained in psychiatric hospitals. Most of the human rights organisations in India do not take up the issues faced by the LGBTQ community. Organisations which have been addressing the issues faced by the LGBTQ community have not addressed it as human rights issue directly, but with issues revolving around HIV and AIDS intervention. The primary reason for doing this has been availability and access to funding through AIDS intervention and fear of directly talking about the issues faced by the community in a country where discussion around sex and sexuality is tabooed. Sometimes, issues related to sexual and gender minorities are even considered as useless issues undertaken by the privileged in the society. Issues of the LGBTQIA community are considered not as important as the issue of poverty, hunger, caste and class oppression and are often seen as a separate issue independent from the structures of social oppression and ideologies of the religious fundamentalism, caste system, patriarchy and capitalism. But the question is how did we reach this point, from having a very progressive NALSA verdict to the tokenistic Transgender (Protection of Rights) Person Bill. Members from the LGBT community have raised their concerns with the NALSA verdict as even though the verdict was progressive, there was room for interpretation. Some members even though that in the absence of a screening community, there would be many individuals who start identifying as transgender to avail protection under the law as homosexuality was criminalised till late 2018. Today, the Indian LGBT community seems divided within themselves with respects to identities and rights that they would stand up for within the spectrum of queer identities.

We had also noticed these debates within the queer community in India especially when the pride march was being planned. There was an intense debate within the community around the representation of queer issues not being independent of intersectionality and structures of social oppression were key discussions of the message and symbolic representations that the pride is to signify to the larger society. A clear divide was seen within the pride planning members' community, with one side feeling that the pride should only cover issues and raise awareness about the issues faced by the LGBT community in India and the other part of the members from the community wanting that emphasis to be laid on the larger structures of social oppression and the way it impacts various identities with queer identity being one of them. There was a small group which felt that they wanted only to represent trans* voices as these voices were not even represented within the queer community. A large part of the LGBT community organising and participating in the Mumbai pride felt that the pride should focus only on the issues directly related to the LGBT community due to the following reasons:

1. Some believed that LGBT issues are separate from the issues of the caste system, patriarchy, capitalism and religious fundamentalism.
2. Other believed that though there is a dependence of LGBT issues with the structures and ideologies of social oppression and did not deny intersectionality—they still wanted LGBT issues to be the only focus of pride as they thought
    (a) Bringing up other issues will only dilute the message around the challenges faced by the LGBT community in the pride march and there would be no clear message around the reasons for the pride march to be taking place. Not only the communication around the LGBT community would have been impacted, but also there would be confusion with regard to the overall message that the pride symbolically represents. Discussions around normative sexuality are still tabooed at most of the places in India, so it becomes essential to have LGBT issues separately for the more significant part of the society, at least at this stage, to make the larger part of the society first understand that LGBT rights are also human rights.

(b) There are laws and advocacy around other issues whereas the LGBT community does not have any or very little protection from the state. It is the need of the hour and very crucial for the community at the present moment to maintain focus on their demands from the state and not talk about all the ill effects caused by the larger structures of oppression of caste system, patriarchy, capitalism and religious fundamentalism all at once, but take one issue at a time.

(c) The most effective way to get any positive result is to take issues separately and once some progress has been made to talk about intersectionality, as social change is a slow and time taking process. Historically the LGBT movements in countries that have equal rights for the community have gone through a similar pattern, and it is not the right time in India to talk about intersectionality academically, but to sensitise individuals from the society so that the entire impact of these campaigning is not diluted.

(d) Some also argued that whenever an instance of hate crime or discrimination takes place or are recorded, they are mostly because of a few primary identities for the discriminator that becomes a reason for discrimination. While there is no disagreement with the role of intersectionality playing a role in most discriminatory practices, the reason for the discrimination to take place are a few primary identities and not all the identities. For instance, when it is said that a transgender individual of colour has been discriminated, it does not mean that this individual or community who is discriminated does not have any other identity, but the primary reason for the individual or the community to be discriminated in this case is for them to be of different skin colour and either self-identifying or "coming across" with the identity of a transgender. Other identities of the individual play a role in discrimination and hate crime, but the impact of these identities becomes secondary. For most of the individuals opposing the discussion of intersectionality during the pride, the primary identity that they have faced discrimination for has been that of gender and sexual orientation identities and thus they would want to address the primary reasons for discrimination and hate crime first which causes them maximum discomfort and is the hardest to deal with rather than addressing issues related to all the identities.

(e) A few also opposed the idea of having discussions around intersectionality as they thought that it would further divide the queer community since different individuals would have different opinions around issues of caste, class, patriarchy and religions and socio-cultural beliefs, thus making it even more difficult for individuals to find common grounds. It would further create differences in ideologies that the pride march would collectively represent. Whereas one thing that all individuals can commonly agree on is that LGBT rights are human rights and that there is a requirement of safe space and laws that protect the right of the LGBT community.
(f) Some also questioned if as LGBT individuals, they can talk about intersectionality and other identities/ideologies that represent minorities—will people belonging to these minorities/ideologies/identities who mostly have normative cis-gender identities support LGBTQ rights and also accept support from the LGBT community even when it is for a common cause, as the community might even be looked down upon the other minorities.

Even with these discussions, there are pride marchers in India, such as the Hyderabad and Delhi pride that have celebrated and had some communication around intersectionality. Whereas the overall vibes for the pride march organisation in Mumbai have been with a focus around only the LGBT issues. This has even lead to the withdrawal of a few individuals and groups from the community from not participating in the pride as according to them the pride has failed to uphold the true spirit of queer movements. For significant individuals from the queer community in India, especially the lesbian, gay and bisexual community, the focus in the pride march and organised protests has been around revocation of Section 377 of the Indian Penal Code. Discussions around equal rights such as the right to marry had not even been started as revocation of Section 377 was considered as the base premise for bringing in other legal reformation thus restricting the focus of the LGB movement in India only till criminalisation under the law. It has only been two months since homosexuality has been decriminalised and we now think that the LGBTQ community would strive towards other rights such as the right to marry, right to ownership of property and right to partner's benefit in the society and in their workplace.

Section 377 of the Indian Penal Code (till September 2018)

Reads as: "Unnatural offences: Whoever voluntarily has carnal intercourse against the order of nature with any man, woman or animal shall be punished with imprisonment for life, or with imprisonment of either description for term which may extend to ten years, and shall also be liable to fine."

The section did not define what qualifies as carnal intercourse which is against the order of nature with any man or woman. Thus, it was assumed and also argued by people who want to keep the section that any other sexual activity between two consulting adults other than peno-vaginal intercourse will be considered against the order of nature. Which means that oral sex or anal intercourse between two consenting heterosexual couple would have also been considered as against the order of nature. The legitimation of peno-vaginal intercourse as being in the order of nature is mainly due to understanding and enforcement of gender and sexuality from the traditional gender model and also from the ability of individuals from opposite normative gender to procreate from the act of peno-vaginal intercourse. So even though the law was to be interpreted to apply to heterosexual couples, it was not in practice for the consenting heterosexual individuals in sexual acts other than peno-vaginal. Most of the people in a heterosexual relationship in India were not even aware that according to this law they can legally only indulge in peno-vaginal intercourse. Then why is it that only people from the LGBTQIA community along with a few allies were protesting against this law?

Majority of the people believe and have believed for a very long time in the traditional gender module for all, thus making heterosexuality a norm. It does not become an issue of concern for the society with regard to which type of sexual activity an adult heterosexual couple may indulge in as a relationship between individuals of the opposite gender is the norm (although the larger society still stigmatises a relationship without marriage). A relationship which is outside the heteronormative structure is not considered acceptable to a large part of the society due to various concerns and stereotypes, thus making such relationships unacceptable. Further, it is not only non-normative relationships that are unacceptable to the larger society but also individuals identifying with gender or sexual orientation that is outside of the traditional gender model. Thus the law, even though was constrained to "carnal intercourse against the order of nature," symbolically was against the existence and identification of individuals who are sexual minorities in India. No individual can be penalised under this section for openly identifying with a non-normative sexual orientation or even for being in a romantic and emotional relationship with a person from the same gender, unless they are involved in carnal intercourse which is against the order of nature. We need to understand that Section 377 did not criminalise a person identifying themselves as homosexuals or identifying with the queer community but only criminalises the sexual activities other than penile-vaginal as a criminal offence; but often, people from the queer community are extorted, molested and even raped on the bases of this section due to their non-normative gender and sexual orientation identity. On February 15, 2014, a gay man was raped by two policemen in Gujarat. Further two gay men were beaten for looking and acting feminine in a restaurant in Bangalore. In both these cases, the victims did not file an FIR for fear of facing further harassment.

There are many other issues with the interpretation of this section. The section is patriarchal as it focuses on the penetration and the power to penetrate. This may lead to an interpretation that women cannot be prosecuted under this law. Further, this section of the law not only covers the act of bestiality but also considers it similar to consenting adults having carnal intercourse against the order of nature. The law is not coherent with the NALSA verdict as there is lack of clarity with regard to participation in carnal intercourse by the transgender community, which is now legally recognised as the "third gender" category, is not against the order of nature. If it is not against the order of nature then what exactly is the criteria for a law to criminalise a particular part of the society on their sexual orientation or a certain act of sexuality.

SECTION 377 OF THE IPC AFTER SEPTEMBER 6, 2018

Everything changed with the revocation of Section 377 in the year 2009 by the Delhi High Court. As per the Delhi High Court judgement, Section 377 violated the fundamental human rights provided under Article 15, 19 and 21 of the Indian Constitution. This judgement was celebrated and welcomed by the LGBTQ and allies, due to various reasons such as the members of the community would no longer be exploited, discriminated and exhorted money on the basis of this law. Further, most of the people the community started believing that at least revocation of the section would lead to decrease in the rate of harassment and discrimination, if not an increase in the rate of acceptance in the society. It was at this point of time that the Indian LGBT community felt motivated that their struggles to attain equal human rights were moving in the right direction. Due to this judgement, many people belonging to the LGBTQ community came out to their families, workplace and overall in society. Further, many from the community started contemplating and planning their coming out journey as they were no longer criminals for being who they are in their own country. Though the case was further challenged in the Supreme Court, the Indian LGBT community was sure that judgement from the Supreme Court will follow the same spirit as the High Court and revoke the law from the Indian Penal Code.

In December 2013, the Supreme Court reintroduced Section 377 by reversing the progressive ruling of the High Court. The Supreme Court's ruling to reintroduce the Section 377 was followed with shock, confusion and fear to the Indian LGBTQ community. After almost a time gap of four year, that is, since the High Court verdict in 2009, the section came back into force. Many people from the community, who came out after the High Court verdict in 2009, were in the most vulnerable situation. The Supreme Court verdict forced many individuals back into the darkness of the closet. Some politicians were also planning to introduce a bill which criminalises an individual who identifies himself/herself/themselves with the Queer Community after the Supreme Court verdict (Singh 2014). Revocation of Section 377 did not mean that the society started accepting the LGBT community, but it provided strength and courage to the community to fight against injustice and discrimination against them. The Supreme Court with reintroducing the section not only criminalised the community again but also took away the rights of the community to express their true identity and the right to fight against injustice and discrimination.

In February 2010, unknown people secretly video recorded a professor in a North Indian university having consensual sex with another man who was a rickshaw puller. The professor had to face a lot of discrimination in the university where he stayed and worked, to the extent that he was forced to leave the university after two months without an inquiry. He was supported by gay rights activities and challenged his sacking to the court. As a result of decriminalisation of consenting sex between two adults by the Delhi High Court in the year 2009, the court stayed the order and the university had to take back the professor on board. Five days after this decision, the professor was found dead in his apartment. The rickshaw puller was arrested by the police thrice. He was harassed and beaten up by the police to such as extent that he attempted self-immolation. Many people belonging to the LGBT community have lost their lives due to constant harassment and discrimination. This horrendous incidence took place after the High Court verdict of 2009 and before the Supreme Court Verdict of 2013. This incident took place at a time when it was not a criminal activity for consenting adults with non-normative gender and/or sexual orientation identities to be involved in a sexual act which was earlier considered as an act against the order of nature.

On September 6, 2018, the Indian queer community celebrated the decriminalisation of homosexual activity between consenting adults as the five bench judge of the Supreme Court legitimised homosexual relationship. However, the question is would change in the law also bring about positive change in the social, cultural and political acceptance of the individuals from the LGBT community by the larger normative part of the society. We had already seen an instance of the professor from a north Indian university being excluded, discriminated and tortured when homosexuality was not considered illegal and immoral in the eye of law after the High Court's verdict.

Even when there are laws to protect the community—the bias against the community is so firmly embedded in the society that the discrimination against the community continues. In the year 2016, an individual, who underwent sexual reassignment surgery (SRS), working with the Indian Navy was realised from the navy on account of her transition. This happened in a time when undergoing SRS is legal in India, and transgender is recognised as a gender category. Further, at a time when the NALSA verdict extends reservation in case of public appointments and admission to the educational institutions for the transgender community in India. Having said this, some positive changes have also come up with the law—such as employment of transgenders in Kerala Metro, and more openness of the society towards initiating difficult conversations around sexuality.

LGBT Community and the Workplace

There have been many pieces of research with regard to the women in organisations and the number of such studies has increased over some time but in most of this research, the identity of the woman is unidimensional as a result of viewing gender from a traditional model. In India when most organisations say that they have a gender diversity and inclusion policy in place, it mostly means that these diversity practices are designed only keeping in mind the women employees. A singular identity of an individual's biological sex that of female forms the basis of these policies, where intersectionality of women's identity is not even taken into consideration, thus making gender diversity practices a synonym of diversity related to women in the organisation. There is a lack of research with regard to the diversity of LGBTQ employees in the workplace, especially in the Indian context. Most of the research around the LGBTQ community in the workplace has been in developed countries such as the US, Canada, UK and the European continent. It is true that the political, legal, economic, socio-cultural and technological conditions of our country are different from that of these developed countries which have relatively more liberal views of the LGBT community. The idea behind using the literature of these countries holds valid even for our country as fundamental human rights, discrimination, violence, harassment and stigma will hold and apply to every human being throughout the world. More research and policies around the LGBTQIA community in these countries does not mean that there are no problems, discrimination and hate crime against the community in these countries. We have already seen at the beginning of this chapter that the hate crime for the LGBT community in the US has been one of the highest of all hate crimes over an elongated period. However, we can learn from these countries as they have already evolved from a similar stage where we are right now with regard to the LGBTQ rights.

Organisations treat people from the LGBT community as abnormal and inferior due to the hostile attitude of the state towards the community (Concannon 2008). As the state does not account same-sex families, even the organisations do not account for equal rights to LGBT employees in the work-family policies (Beauregard et al. 2007). This makes sexual orientation diversity one of the least important factors that organisations outside the US take into consideration (Goodman 2013).

The sexual orientation of employees are assumed to be apparent to all the other employees, but this assumption may not always be correct as given the fact that sexual orientation is invisible in nature and that it can be easily concealed by homosexual individuals (Ragins and Wiethoff 2005). Lesbian and gay employees in the organisations are expected to behave and confirm with the hegemonic discourse which requires them to express themselves in a heteronormative way (Burton and Bairstow 2013). Ragins and Wiethoff (2005) founded that there might be a difference in the self-perceived image of the gay men with that of straight men, as gay men may not identify with straight men. The same might be true for lesbian women identifying with straight women. Implicit Inversion theory is often used to understand how a feeling of difference between the LGBT communities arises as compared to the heterosexual population. According to the implicit inversion theory people from the LGBT community, primarily gay and lesbian individuals, challenge the traditional gendered role.

The household specialisation model suggests that the skill level of a person is directly related to the amount of compensation that person is likely to earn (Allegretto and Arthur 2001; Badgett 1995; Becker 1993; Black et al. 2003; Carpenter 2005; Clain and Leppel 2001; Klawitter and Flatt 1998). This means that lesbian women may earn a higher amount of compensation as compared to heterosexual women, at the same time, gay men would earn less compensation as compared to his straight male counterpart. The reason behind this is lesbian women will have more time to focus on their career. Further, the probability of lesbian women as compared to heterosexual women to take a break in their career due to childbirth is less thus giving her an edge to move ahead in her career. The level of masculinity defines workplace success as workplaces are designed to fit the lifestyle of a man. Due to all the factors, a lesbian woman may come across as more masculine and suited at the workplace as compared to that of a heterosexual woman. Similarly, a gay man may be considered less masculine and is likely to earn less as compared to a cis-gender heterosexual man. Recent research conducted by Martell and Roncolato (2016) suggests that for gay and lesbian women with children there is a concave relationship between relative earnings and the time spent on household labour. This study suggests that sexual orientation and gender identity have an impact on the economic outcomes even when the findings are inconstant with the household model.

These research findings become vital as we understand that gender and sexual orientation of an individual impacts the economic outcomes even in countries with equal marriage rights for the LGBT individuals. In countries like India, where laws like Section 377 have prevailed until very recent times, one could easily assume that for most people from the community there is a higher negative economic as well as mental wellbeing impact of the non-normative gender and sexual orientation identity, especially if these identities are visible. It is difficult to come out for most of the individuals from the community due to the fear of rejection and discrimination. During the research, we have met several lesbian and gay individuals who are married to people from the opposite gender to lead a normative life as they feared coming out. For these individuals, coming out with their real identity has not been an option, thus making them remain in a forced marriage with a partner who has a heterosexual identity. Studies around the household specialisation or bargaining model do not take into consideration lesbian and gay individuals who hide their non-normative sexual orientation and perform as heterosexuals to be in a heterosexual marriage for the fear and repercussions caused due to coming out. Since the sexual orientation of the individuals is invisible, most individuals from the community who are cis-gender can pass as straight and thus avoid the stigma.

People who consider homosexuality as immoral and want to not only keep Section 377 but also bring in harder anti-LGBT laws, often argue that giving rights to the LGBT community would spread immorality in the society. According to these people, giving recognition and equal marriage rights to the LGBT community would lead to a conversation of straight people into individuals with LGBT identity. Thus, their argument for keeping the regressive laws is to curb the spread of immorality in the society. These people do not understand that not having equal rights and respect leads many people from the community to not come out with their non-normative identities. From these people who are not out, many become part of a heterosexual relationship or marriage due to the immense pressure to conform. It affects not only the people from the community but also the lives of their heterosexual partner who is not aware of the non-normative sexual orientation identity of the person they are married to or are in a relationship with. It might also happen that the individuals from the community who are in a heterosexual marriage are secretly living their non-normative sexual orientation identity and are in a sexual relationship with multiple partners thus raising the risk of sexually transmitted disease (STD). Thus not having equal rights, not giving respect, recognition for the LGBT community in the society is expected to cause more problems in the society, and these problems are not only problems related with regard to the economic outcome of the individual but also problems related to public health and social structures in the society.

A study was conducted by Kristen Schilt and Matthew Wiswall (2008) where M2F (male to female) and F2M (female to male) trans-people's compensation before and after the sexual reassignment surgery (SRS) were noted. It was observed that the trans-person who had converted himself from F2M received a higher amount of compensation after the surgery whereas the trans-person who had converted herself from M2F, witnessed a fall in her compensation. So far, we have emphasised non-normative gender and sexual orientation identity causing discrimination in the hiring process, at the workplace and regarding overall career growth. From this research on transsexual individuals' transition and its impact on their compensation to the research around household specialisation model, we come to know that organisations have been very masculine. Gender imbalance is witnessed in most of the organisations throughout the world. This imbalance increases as we go higher in the organisational hierarchy. This is only in context with the representation of women in the organisations. Representation of LGBTQ individuals in the organisation, especially in the leadership position, is visible only in a handful of Indian organisations.

According to Katherine Franke and MacKinnon (taken from Butler 1999), production of gender is the primary goal of gender hierarchy, and it is because of sexual harassment that gender hierarchy is created. We have to understand that not all the discrimination related to gender may be harassment. The act of harassment is one where a person from is made to behave in a certain way to comply with the gendered role laid down by society. People from the LGBT community may be discriminated at their workplace as they would fail to appear similar to their straight counterparts. This illusionary appearance becomes the reality of our lives. For instance, how men and women dress is a perfect example of an illusion of appearance. If a man dresses like a woman, this illusion is challenged, leading not only to discrimination but also to harassment. Here the word "appear" does not only means the physical appearance due to clothing, as it might be controlled in most of the organisations by way of a dress code, but the way persons from LGBT community present themselves to other employees, clients and customers. Thus, discrimination and sexual harassment of the people from the queer community is due to not only the prevalence of gender hierarchy but also the attempt to have gender normativity, where the norms driven around masculinity leads to the acceptance of one gender above another due to political laws and natural laws guided by the ethical believes of a society.

Masculinity can be divided into two categories which are orthodox masculinity and inclusive masculinity. Orthodox masculinity is based on three fundamental principles which are homophobia, misogyny and excessive risk-taking. According to Messner (1992), orthodox masculinity, which drives homophobia, is used as a tool to express heterosexuality which is considered superior by the society. Indian culture does not segregate gender from sexuality. For instance, during the research, many gay respondents reported that most of the time transgenders and gay men are believed to be the same in India. Further, we also commonly use stereotypes such as all gay men are effeminate and that all men who have feminine characteristics are also gay.

The majority of Indian organisations subscribe to the ideology of orthodox masculinity. Even the reinstatement of Section 377 and the reasons given for reinstating this law is a result of orthodox masculine thought of the two bench judges making this decision. Similarly, it is a common stereotype that lesbian women are "butch" or showcasing an extreme form of masculinity. However, moderate display of masculinity by women is generally not stereotyped as people in our country have a great craving for a male child and also due to another stereotype of women appearing masculine being able to protect themselves or/and not attract attention which may lead to problems such as sexual harassment and rape. But interestingly, masculinity in women to a certain extent is accepted by the society and the family members proudly, till a certain age—and this is the age till the woman is considered eligible for marriage. A similar kind of environment can easily be witnessed in organisations where people at the top management belief in orthodox masculinity. It is this kind of corporate culture which is not accepting of alternate sexualities and gender identities and does not give equal opportunity to women. In such societies or organisations, if one wishes to escape homosexual stigma, then they participate in either in the hetero-masculine environment (Pronger 1990) or men sexually objectifying women (Hughson 2000) along with women romanticising men. Men often sexually degrade women to prove their heterosexuality and masculinity, and this does not only include heterosexual men. In our research, we had noticed that even gay men who are not out in their organisation might participate in sexual degradation or objectification of women to appear more masculine at the workplace.

The concept of inclusive masculinity was first used by Anderson (2009), where he defined the term as a social process concerning the emergence of an archetype of masculinity that undermines the principles of orthodox masculine values. In his book, *Inclusive Masculinity: The Changing Nature of Masculinity*, Anderson described the relationship between reduction in cultural homophobia and the effect of this reduction on hegemonic masculine heterosexuals. Men at the bottom of the hierarchy look up to men at the top of the hierarchy and follow the type of masculinity practised by these men at the top of the hierarchy. In organisations where men at the top are homophobic, rejection and stigmatisation of people with alternate sexual orientation and gender are higher as people at the lower level also feel that their actions are justified as they are only obliged to their seniors.

In an organisation, institution or culture where inclusive masculinity is followed, employees feel more social freedom when it comes to the expression of their behaviour and attitudes. In a culture where extreme homophobia is witnessed only one archetype of masculinity domination exists, whereas in a culture where homophobia is decreasing multiple archetypes of masculinity is witnessed. In an inclusive masculine culture, the dominance of a type of masculinity is decided by the majority of people subscribing to a school of thought and not by the hegemonic dominance. Thus, in a culture of inclusive masculinity, dominance of one type of masculinity thought is not felt as there is no hegemonic dominance. According to Swain (2006a, 2006b), in a culture where inclusive masculinity is present, men can subscribe to the masculinity they desire without undergoing a cultural pull. Further, Ibson (2002) also described that in such a culture, homo-socially speaking that is tactile and softer forms of masculinity will flourish.

According to Goffman (1963), people forming the majority, view the minority as non-normal and often stigmatise them. The corporate jobs are structured in such a way that it suits the lifestyle of "a man" and that men majorly dominate most of the professions today. This is because in our society the man is still considered the primary breadwinner, works hard in the office and then goes back home where his wife, who is the home bearer, satisfies all his needs. The dominance of men in the workforce is a result of a very old stereotype existing from hundreds of years—that of men being physically more stronger compared to women and thus being preferred fit for being the providers to the family in different eras through hunting, agriculture and work in industries and organisations. Throughout history, we have seen that women had to go through so many problems in the society and the organisations, and the major reason behind this was that women were never considered as gender equal compared to the "Men." Women have always been the second or the other gender. Even today, we are talking about equality in wages/salary for men and women in the workplace doing similar kind of work.

Similarly, the LGBT community also faces problems in the organisation. Exclusion, discomfort, stereotyping and formation of a fractured identity by other people in the organisation have been witnessed by the employees identifying with the LGBT community (Roberts 2011). This community is looked at as the "third gender" which is even a grade below than that of the women, or even worse, when not considered to be a part of the heteronormative gender binary by many individuals and societies. Thus, we have seen that organisations have been very hetero-sexist, masculine and patriarchal. This feeling of "other" (Ragins 2008) or the fear of having a courtesy stigma from the society has also prevented many individuals from associating with the LGBT community (Deitch et al. 2004). Employees from LGBT community would consciously take the first step towards coming out at the workplace only when organisations are create a support system of co-workers who accept and respect the gender identity and sexual orientation of these employees (The Lesbian Almanac 1996, taken from Griffith and Hebl 2002).

Most of the researches on LGBT employees in the workplace have concentrated on either discrimination in the form of selection and differential pay to the sexual minorities or issues related to flow of information related to sexual orientation at the workplace (Roberts 2011). According to a study conducted by Becker (1971), employees from the minority group are hired in the organisation so that the employer can fulfil their "taste" of discrimination against them. People from the LGBT community may work in a lower paying occupation if the work environment allows them to be open about their orientation. So their opportunity cost would be a higher paying job where the traditional gender model is the norm. Further, according to Ellis and Riggle (1995), gay men and lesbian women were more likely to choose an occupation in an industry which is more open and accepting of the LGBT community. They also identified that gay men might take up jobs which were identified with the female identity. All of the above could be the reasons for people from the LGBT community to earn lower compensation as compared to their heterosexual counterparts. We have explored these questions in detail in the coming chapters to get a comprehensive understanding of the narratives prevalent in the Indian context.

LGBT trade union and network groups play an essential role in bringing up and solving various issues faced by LGBT employees in countries where people from the LGBT community have equal rights. These trade unions and networking groups in organisations give visibility to LGBT employees (Colgan and McKcarnery 2012). Despite the presence of these trade unions and networking groups, diversity and inclusion policies fail to translate in the work culture leading to an implementation gap even in these countries. The fact that LGBT employees in these countries are aware of the existence of these support systems acts as one of the relief systems even to individuals who have not come out of the closet. Though LGBT employees look up to the leaders in the top and middle management to provide proactive leadership and reduce the implementation gap (Colgan et al. 2007), leadership remains the domain of heterosexual patriarchy (Gedro 2010).

A foreign bank operating in India had approached us as they wanted support on the diversity and inclusion issues of the LGBT employees for their Indian Office. We spoke to the marketing and human resource head of this organisation on the issues faced by the Indian LGBT community and the way their organisation can play an instrumental role by introducing diversity and inclusion initiatives and policies that will not only benefit the LGBT community and their employees but also help the organisation development in a positive direction. We could understand that the marketing head was not keen on having these diversity and inclusion policy because she thought that neither these policies were required in compliance with any law, but also there was Section 377 which was against the community during that time. This became a good excuse for the organisation to not take upon the inclusion and diversity initiatives as they were considered unrequired and excess work. We explained to these leaders the interpretation of Section 377 of IPC that it does not withhold any organisation from having a diversity and inclusion policy in their organisation for the LGBT community nor stops any individual from openly identifying with the queer community multiple times. We further educated this client about the fundamental rights laid by the constitution, the NALSA verdict and the Right to privacy law. However, the marketing head kept pointing out one or another reason for not having these policies. Further, the reasons given for not having these policies kept changing from Section 377 to the assumption that the union will not be able to digest such policies, to the misinformation about identifying and carrying any activities related to such diversity initiatives. As far as the union was concerned, these leaders thought that members of the union will not be able to understand this decision taken by the organisation as they were not as "evolved" as the management. There are very few organisations in India who are openly talking about the issues of the LGBT community; these organisations have not faced any resistance from the union so far to not have such inclusive policies. Since we have not interacted with the members of unions in the organisations about the issues faced by LGBT employees, it would be difficult for us to list out the reasons for which the union will or may have reacted in organisations which has diversity and inclusion policy versus the organisations which do not have them. Our understanding of one of the primary functions for the union is to have justice and higher collective bargaining for the worker's welfare and that these policies and initiatives would ultimately lead to an environment that is more accepting. Creating an environment where people from the LGBT community can integrate themselves benefits not only the employees but also the organisation (Colgan and McKcarnery 2012). Workplace friendship may help the LGBT managers to negotiate managerial identities and overcome career obstacles (Rumens 2011). Griffith and Hebl (2002) reported that LGBT employees, who disclosed their identity and worked for an organisation which was gay-friendly, reported higher job satisfaction and lower levels of anxiety.

REFERENCES

Allegretto, S.A., and M.M. Arthur. 2001. *Industrial and Labor Relations Review* 54 (3): 631–646.

Anderson, E. 2009. *Inclusive Masculinity: The Changing Nature of Masculinities.* Routledge.

Badgett, M.V. 1995. The Wage Effects of Sexual-Orientation Discrimination. *Industrial and Labor Relations Review* 48 (4): 726–739.

Beauregard, T.A., et al. 2007. Revisiting the Social Construction of Family in the Context of Work. *Journal of Managerial Psychology* 24 (1): 46–65.

Becker, Gary. 1971. *The Economics of Discrimination.* Chicago: University of Chicago Press.

Becker, G.S. 1993. The Economic Way of Looking at Behaviour. *The Journal of Political Economy* 101 (3): 385–409.

Black, D.A., H.R. Makar, S.G. Sanders, and L.J. Taylor. 2003. The Effects of Sexual Orientation on Earnings. *Industrial and Labor Relations Review* 56 (3): 449–469.

Burton, H.W., and S. Bairstow. 2013. Countering Heteronormativity: Exploring the Negotiation of Butch Lesbian Identity in the Organisational Setting. *Gender in Management: An International Journal* 28 (6): 359–374.

Butler, J. 1999. *Gender Trouble.* New York: Routledge Press.

Carpenter, Christopher. 2005. Self-Reported Sexual Orientation and Earnings: Evidence from California. *Industrial and Labor Relations Review, ILR Review, Cornell University, ILR School* 58 (2): 258–273.

Clain, S.H., and K. Leppel. 2001. An Investigation into Sexual Orientation Discrimination as an Explanation for Wage Differences. *Applied Economics* 33: 37–47.

Colgan, F., and A. McKcarnery. 2012. Visibility and Voice in Organisations Lesbian, Gay, Bisexual and Transgender Employee Networks. *Equality Diversity and Inclusion: An International Journal* 31 (4): 359–378.

Colgan, F., et al. 2007. Equality and Diversity Policies and Practices at Work: Lesbian, Gay and Bisexual Workers. *Equal Opportunities International* 26 (6): 590–609.

Concannon, L. 2008. Citizenship, Sexual Identity and Social Exclusion: Exploring Issues in British and American Social Policy. *International Journal of Sociology and Social Policy* 28 (9/10): 326–339.

Connell, R.W. 1998. Masculinities and Globalization. *Men and Masculinities* 1 (1): 3–23.

Deitch, E.A., R.M. Butz, and A.P. Brief. 2004. Out of the Closet and Out of the Job? The Nature, Import, and Causes of Sexual Orientation Discrimination in the Workplace. In *The Dark Side of Organizational Behaviour*, ed. R. Griffin and A. O'Leary-Kelly. San Francisco, CA: Jossey-Bass.

Ellis, A.L., and E.D.B. Riggle. 1995. The Relation of Job Satisfaction and Degree of Openness About One's Sexual Orientation for Lesbian and Gay Men. *Journal of Homosexuality* 30: 75–85.

Foucault, M. 1976. *The History of Sexuality. Vol. 1: An Introduction*. Trans. Robert Hurley. Penguin.

Gedro, J. 2010. Lesbian Presentations and Representations of Leadership and the Implications for HRD. *Journal of European Industrial Training* 34 (6): 552–564.

Goffman, Erving. 1963. *Stigma*. London: Penguin.

Goodman, N.R. 2013. Taking Diversity and Inclusion Initiatives Global. *Industrial and Commercial Training* 45 (3): 180–183.

Griffith, K.H., and M.R. Hebl. 2002. The Disclosure Dilemma for Gay Men and Lesbians: "Coming Out" at Work. *Journal of Applied Psychology* 87: 1191–1199.

Hughson, J. 2000. The Boys Are Back in Town: Soccer Support and the Social Reproduction of Masculinity. *Journal of Sport and Social Issues* 24: 8–23.

Ibson, J. 2002. *Picturing Men: A Century of Male Relationships in Everyday Life*. Washington, DC: Smithson Books.

Klawitter, M.M., and V. Flatt. 1998. The Effects of State and Local Antidiscrimination Policies on Earnings for Gays and Lesbians. *Journal of Policy Analysis and Management* 17 (4): 658–686.

Martell, M.E., and L. Roncolato. 2016. The Homosexual Lifestyle: Time Use in Same-Sex Households. *Journal of Demographic Economics* 82 (4): 365–398.

Messner, M. 1992. *Power at Play: Sports and the Problem of Masculinity*. Boston: Beacon Press.

Pronger, B. 1990. Gay Jocks: A Phenomenology of Gay Men in Athletics. In *Sport, Men and the Gender Order: Critical Feminist Perspectives*, ed. M.A. Messner and D.F. Sabo, 141–152. Champaign, IL: Human Kinetics Books.

Ragins, B.R. 2008. Disclosure Disconnects: Antecedents and Consequences of Disclosure Invisible Stigma Across Life Domains. *Academy of Management Review* 33 (1): 194–215.

Ragins, B.R., and C. Wiethoff. 2005. Understanding Heterosexism at Work: The Straight Problem. In *Discrimination at Work: Psychological and Organizational Bases*, ed. R.L. Dipboye and A. Colella, 177–201. Mahwah, NJ: Lawrence Erlbaum Associates.

Roberts, S. 2011. Exploring How Gay Men Manage Their Social Identities in the Workplace: The Internal/External Dimensions of Identity. *Equality Diversity and Inclusion: An International Journal* 30 (8): 668–685.

Rumens, N. 2011. Minority Support: Friendship and the Development of Gay and Lesbian Managerial Careers and Identities. *Equality Diversity and Inclusion: An International Journal* 30 (6): 444–462.

Schilt, K., and M. Wiswall. 2008. Before and After: Gender Transitions, Human Capital, and Workplace Experiences. *The B.E. Journal of Economic Analysis & Policy* 8 (1): 1–28.

Singh, Sukhdeep. 2014, December 14. *BJP MP from Bikaner to Table Anti-Homosexuality Bill in Lok Sabha*. http://www.gaylaxymag.com/latest-news/bjp-mp-from-bikaner-to-table-anti-homosexuality-bill-in-lok-sabha/. Accessed 15 December 2014.

Swain, J. 2006a. The Role of Sport in the Construction of Masculinities in an English Independent Junior School. *Sport, Education and Society* 11: 317–335.

———. 2006b. Reflections on Patterns of Masculinity in School Settings. *Men and Masculinities* 8: 331–349.

The Immigration and Refugee Board of Canada. 2009. *Situations of Homosexuals: Availability of Support Group and State Protection*. Ottawa.

CHAPTER 2

Accepted as the Other: Discrimination, Identity Crises and Coping Mechanism

Before we deep dive into the discriminatory instances faced by the LGBTQ employees, let us look at the following verbatim. These verbatims will give us a clear understanding of two essential aspects:

1. What qualifies as discrimination?
2. Who decides if a person has been discriminated?

Verbatim 1: *People would call you Hijra, guud; show favouritism in a different way. The discrimination might not be very blatant, might not be in your face. People might not say that oh you know what he is a fag and let's not speak to him or let's not give him work to do but in their own way, they would start playing favouritism. They would look down upon you.* A gay man

Verbatim 2: *I mean there is a certain amount of discrimination towards us… and it's not necessarily discrimination in direct form, but people tend to be discriminating in a variety of ways. I mean they judge you, your professional ability, you know, it seems that you are not a serious applicant because of the fact that you are transgender.* A transgender man

You have to now pause and think about these cases. Which of these cases qualify as discrimination and what is the reason behind it? Further, also think if there is any difference and/or similarities in these cases.

Discrimination against LGBTQ individuals within the workplace context can be broadly defined as biased or prejudicial treatment of employees/

employers due to their sexual orientation, gender identity and gender performativity resulting in the denial of opportunity or unfair treatment. Instances of discrimination are limited to not only the employees working in the organisation but also individuals who are applying for a position in the organisation. Further, discriminatory acts and indifferent attitude are not just limited to the employees of an organisation or any representative of an organisation. It is also applicable to other stakeholders of the organisation which includes members of the civil society, competitors and the government body. For instance, if the advertisement campaign of an organisation is homophobic and/or transphobic—it will be considered as hate speech or discrimination towards the LGBTQ population of a nation (depending on the law of the land and the way a nation views its LGBTQ population).

The sexual orientation of employees are assumed to be apparent to all the other employees, but this assumption may not always be true as sexual orientation is invisible and it can be easily concealed by homosexual individuals (Ragins and Wiethoff 2005). This is because the majority of our society is still following the traditional gender model (discussed in Chap. 1). Unless an individual is visibly queer (not cis-gender) or has not disclosed their identity, they would be automatically assumed to be either male or female depending on their biological sex and gender performativity. Lesbian and gay employees in the organisations are expected to behave and confirm with the hegemonic discourse which requires them to express themselves in a heteronormative way (Burton and Bairstow 2013). Ragins and Wiethoff (2005) found that there might be a difference in the self-perceived image of gay men with that of straight men, as gay men may not identify with straight men. The same might be true for lesbian women identifying with straight women.

During our research, we found that most of the participants experienced discrimination in their workplace. Discrimination at the workplace for LGBTQ employees can broadly be categorised as non-verbal, verbal and physical.

Non-Verbal Discrimination

This was the most reported form of discrimination by our participants. Most of the time, the discrimination might not be very blatant. Almost all the participants expect a few closeted individuals, who passed as cis-gender in their organisation, have felt an indifferent attitude by other colleagues and, at times, by even customers. Often individuals from the community find it difficult to form a bond or connection with their colleagues resulting in the feeling of isolation. Imagine spending an entire day working with people who are indifferent towards you, who would avoid conversations or any contact with you, who would not want to talk or sit with you during lunch. Body language and actions of people may not always lead to verbal, non-verbal or physical discrimination, but it still sends a message to various LGBTQ individuals that they are not wanted. Most LGBTQ individuals try to avoid thinking about these situations even though they very often experience it. Some individuals have also reported that they have got used to the negative attitude of people towards them and that it has become a part of their lives. Few have even added that they are fortunate to face only non-verbal discrimination and an indifferent attitude and not verbal discrimination or physical assault that they might have or are facing in other spaces of society. Bias in the form of non-verbal discrimination for the LGBTQ community not only leads to the feeling of exclusion but also affects their professional growth that is formed due to the halo effect of their non-normative gender and sexual orientation identity. It is not only a personal struggle for the LGBTQ community, but it also affects the productivity of the team and the organisation. The solution is not for people to become overtly friendly towards the LGBTQ community to make them feel a part of the group, but one should be mindful of their bias and how these biases are reflected in not only their speech and action but also their body language. Acknowledging that each one of us is unique and yet we have many similarities is the first step towards addressing our own biases.

Non-verbal discrimination is one of the most difficult to detect in an organisation and even when it is detected, it is not considered as a serious issue. Individuals from the LGBTQ community working in organisations which have inclusion and diversity policies have faced an indifferent attitude from their colleagues. Non-verbal and verbal discrimination may even take place in organisations which have inclusive policies for the LGBTQ employees. In an organisation which has an inclusive policy, even though everyone in the organisation may be aware that they cannot discriminate against the LGBTQ employees as it is not in line with the organisations value and culture, individuals from the community could still feel a lack of acceptance as people would maintain distance and, also, it would show in their non-verbal communication/behaviour. Often individuals working in organisations which have inclusion and diversity policy have not reported non-verbal discrimination to the authorities as they feel that it will come across as a petty issue and would not be taken seriously.

Thus, most of the individuals from the community have to "deal" with such situations.

The first verbatim discussed in the beginning of this chapter is an example of non-verbal and verbal discrimination along with the indifferent attitude of employees towards this individual who has not disclosed his non-normative sexual orientation but is visibly queer. Let us see a case which will help us understand instances of non-verbal discrimination.

Case 1: Rekha is a transsexual woman undergoing transformation. She has been taking hormones since the past one year and is soon planning to undergo surgery. Before she came out, she was working with an international IT firm located in Hyderabad. After the SC passed the NALSA verdict, Rekha decided that now would be a good time to come out as the law was supporting the rights of transgender individuals in India. With a lot of courage, she came out in her organisation as a transsexual woman. She thought that she would be supported by her organisation as it was an international organisation which promoted diversity and inclusion even for LGBTQ individuals in their head office located in the US. Even before she realised, she was given a termination letter. The reason cited in the termination letter was not related to her being transsexual but towards her poor performance. Rekha was in shock as her performance had never been an issue in the last seven years that she had worked in the organisation. She decided to take the matter ahead with the higher authorities of the organisation but did not get any support. Ultimately, she had to leave the organisation.

She decided that now that she was out and had disclosed her identity, there was no going back for her. She decided to disclose her identity to the organisation that she would be working with, to avoid problems at a later stage. On her resume, she had mentioned that she identifies as a transsexual woman undergoing the process of transformation and is seeking for an equal opportunity employer. It has been almost a year she has been looking for a job. Most of the organisations would not even communicate that she has not received the offer or the reason for which they rejected her. However, this is not surprising as the majority of the organisations do not communicate to the applicants if they have been rejected for a role. Few organisations which communicated about her rejection would give the reason that either her skills did not match the job requirement or they found another candidate who was more suitable for the role. Before the transformation process had started, she had never faced so many rejections and getting a call for an interview was not so difficult.

After numerous attempts, she has received a call for the first round of interview from an international IT company which is known for its diversity and inclusion practices. She was very excited as this was also her dream company that she always wanted to work for. She had high hopes to get this job as she had managed to clear the first round of the interview and the human resource manager who had taken the interview was very receptive and friendly.

She has been called for the second round with a senior official in the organisation. Rekha entered the cabin of this senior official and reached out to shake hands with the person who was taking her interview. The person refused to shake hand with her, and the interview did not last more than 5 minutes. She felt insulted and decided that she will write about her experience to the diversity and inclusion team of the organisation. The diversity and inclusion team of the organisation were quick to respond and apologised for what she had to go through. They even promised in their email that they would conduct a sensitivity programme for all their employees in the organisation so that such incidents will not be repeated in future.

Rekha has still not been able to find a job.

VERBAL DISCRIMINATION

After non-verbal discrimination, a majority of the participants have reported facing verbal discrimination. Gay and transgender individuals who were either out, in transition and/or were visibly queer reported being verbally discriminated to a much larger extent compared to lesbians, bisexuals and cis-gender queer individuals at their workplace. Most of the lesbian women that were interviewed reported that the extent of derogatory remarks faced by them was much higher by their cis-gender female colleges as compared to their male counterparts. Not that their male colleges did not discriminate against them, but it is due to result of the culture where people from the opposite gender are expected to be maintaining a distance or boundary thus limiting their interaction with the opposite gender. In India, we often hear about formal and informal groups and authorities harassing heterosexual unmarried couples in public places such as parks. The expectations to maintain the boundary is ingrained in our society from a very young age. Even today in most of the Indian co-education schools, we can see segregation in the sitting arrangements for boys and girls in the same classroom. Gender-based segregation can be seen in all the structures of our society from our own house to the workplace, thus reminding us time and again the boundaries that one gender needs to maintain towards another gender. As a result of which, women with lesbian identity have reported that they have sensed more non-verbal discrimination and a difference in the attitude from their male colleagues as the communication of the same directly towards them in form of verbal communication gets limited to the cultural boundary. Thus, if a woman is to be verbally discriminated by a man in the workplace would depend on the closeness in their relationship and the power relationship between them. The discrimination, be it verbal or non-verbal, is explicit and is more significant from their cis-gender female colleges in the workplace. The same was also reported by some of the gay men who were not cis-gender or had feminine attributes. Further, some of these gay men who did not conform as cis-gender also reported that even though their female colleges were biased, the acceptance of their identity was much higher by their female colleges as compared to their male colleagues. The primary reason for the same was lower levels of assumed sexual tension due to more and visible feminine attributes in these non-cis-gender gay men which resulted in blurring the cultural boundary that exists for cis-gender heterosexual individuals from the opposite sex. Further, just the act (thought) of associating with feminine men was thought to be affecting the masculinity of cis-gender heterosexual male colleagues.

Just like non-verbal discrimination, most of the LGBTQ employees have tried to avoid situations by ignoring verbal discrimination and derogatory comments. Even though most of the individuals wanted to report these instances, have avoided derogatory remarks explicitly made towards them and had tried to turn a blind eye towards these situations, as they were either not sure of an existing mechanism in their workplace to tackle such situations or feared that the situation would only get worse for them if it were to be reported. Very few individuals, even from those who have been out in their organisation, have been able to confront such situations and when these instances were formally reported, the situation was not handled appropriately by their organisation. Some have even lost their job or had to leave the organisation after reporting the incident, as instead of addressing the root cause of the issue the organisations have thought that it would be "less work" for them and better to get rid of individuals who do not conform with the organisational and societal norms.

A trans-man working with an organisation in Mumbai had undergone severe depression for three years as a result of the shock from the verbal discrimination which led to his identity crises. This was a result of repeated derogatory remarks and prejudice against him at the workplace along with lack of support system. After he quit the job at the organisation where he had to face these remarks day in and day out, he developed a phobia for working in an organisation as he feared that he would be treated the same way in any other organisation.

Case 2: You are the human resource manager of an organisation, and an incident of indecent workplace behaviour has been reported to you. The narrative of the aggrieved individual is as follows. How will you tackle this problem?

1. Assume that Mr X is a heterosexual cis-gender man and the aggrieved person reporting this incidence is a heterosexual cis-gender woman. What would your reaction as an HR in the organisation be?

   Mr X has a lot of problems and I don't know why he had problems with me. Today we had a huge fight as in a very big argument. He got offended. He just raised his voice and said 'you are a girl that's why it's okay otherwise I would have slapped you' this is the worst thing that I have ever heard.

2. Will there be any change in your decision if the gender of the aggrieved person was to be that of a transsexual individual who was informally out in the organisation?
3. Will you change your decision if both Mr X and the aggrieved person were to be heterosexual women?

Now let us look at the complete verbatim of the transgender person who left his job, developed a phobia for working in any other organisation and dealt with chronic depression for three years after leaving his job.

Mr X has a lot of problems and I don't know why he had problems with me. We had a huge fight as in a very big argument. He got offended. He just raised his voice and said 'you are a girl that's why it's okay otherwise I would have slapped you' this is the worst thing that I have ever heard. Even if I was a man or a woman or any gender a senior has no right to talk to their junior like that. Forget seniors and juniors, but you cannot talk like this to your colleagues in an organisational setup. When my bosses came to know about the whole incidence they did not take any action. The boss just said to my senior that 'you have lost respect in my eyes.' But this does not make any difference. He should have been fired. First of all, you insulted me calling a 'woman' when I identify as a transman. At least you should have used the word 'tom' boy, you can argue, fight but should never go on the gender of a person. Even after this incident, he kept teasing me and calling me a girl. Not only did my immediate senior insulted me by calling me a woman time and again but also they degraded my work profile. He made me stand at the airport with a placard to pick up people from the airport. That is not my job profile. When they told me to do this I just left the placard and left that was my resignation. I did not give them an official resignation.

PHYSICAL DISCRIMINATION AND SEXUAL HARASSMENT

Comparatively, instances of physical abuse and sexual harassment for the members of the community were reported to be higher in other spaces of the society as compared to their workplace. However, few participants also reported to physical and sexual harassment at their workplace. Physical discrimination and sexual harassment at the workplace was accompanied with verbal and non-verbal discrimination.

Case 3: Your friend is physically harassed as a result of his effeminate behaviour by his colleagues at his workplace. He seeks your advice to tackle the situation. He does not want to provide any information to his employers that will directly or indirectly reveal his identity as a gay person. Go through the narrative below and give advice your friend on the best way to handle this situation.

> *Sometimes few guys will come and touch my back inappropriately. I really feel bad then I ignore, and I let them do anything. I do not know if they are doing it just for fun, but I feel bad. I am like why to make this a big issue but if I do something like this to a girl how will she feel but we don't have any guidelines for the LGBT people, so I cannot complain anywhere. We do have an anti-discrimination policy but that is only for women. It does not include LGBT.* A gay man

In the above case, we can see that a closeted gay man is physically harassed at his workplace by his colleagues due to his effeminate behaviour. This individual feels that he has no choice but to avoid and ignore the situations which makes him uncomfortable almost every other day at his workplace. Even in organisations which have inclusion and diversity policies for the LGBTQ employees, closeted individuals avoid reporting these instances. Most of the time, the individuals ignore these situations thus giving a signal to the perpetrator that they can continue with similar actions. Further, the larger society turns a blind eye towards such instances. In Indian society, we have sexual harassment law in the workplace that is meant only to address the problems of individuals whose gender assigned at birth is that of female. Having sexual harassment law only for the women which is titled as "The Sexual Harassment of Women at Workplace (Prevention, Prohibition and Redressal) Act 2013," either implies that only women in our society can be sexually harassed, or men are masculine enough to handle such situations on their own and thus do not require any law. We believe that women in Indian society are more vulnerable and thus we require laws to protect, but it does not imply that there should be no provision for the protection of all gender and sexual orientations under the law. Irrespective of their gender—any individuals can be harassed by other individuals from the same or different gender category. The law which protects women against only men is also a result of heteronormativity in our society.

What would have happened if the above incident had taken place with a woman being the victim and touched inappropriately by a male colleague? Would the result of the same discrimination be different if the discriminator was a woman and had touched a man inappropriately irrespective of his sexual orientation? Would the man in such a situation be in a position to file a complaint? Would his complaint be taken seriously? Also, how would the case take shape if a woman would have conducted such kind of physical assault on another woman? Though in all the questions, the discriminatory instance is considered to be the same, the way discrimination would have been tackled would be different because of the masculinity, femininity and politics of the human body and gender identity attached with the victim and the abuser in the incidence. It is because of this attitude that the majority of people in our country think that men cannot be raped, sexually exploited or molested by other or the same gender. Though now the legal definition of "rape" has changed, it is still believed by many that women cannot be molested or raped by another woman because of her incapability to penetrate with a penis. This is also the reason that Section 377 of the IPC may not apply to consenting adult women due to their inability to penetrate as a result of their biological sex.

Victims of sexual harassment which does not fall in the normative category of a woman being harassed by a man are often confused and fear talking about these experience. Having gender-neutral laws for protection, prevention and redressal of sexual harassment will send a message to the society that irrespective of the gender identity and sexual orientation of the person—the act of sexual harassment is condemned. Gender-neutral laws may not drastically increase the number of cases reported by individuals of the LGBTQ community in the initial years of its introduction or even by heterosexual men but will strengthen the value of equality and fraternity. Here is another instance of sexual harassment faced during a business trip by a closeted gay man:

> *Once I was off-site, where I was sent with a colleague from another department and we had to stay in one of the room. An hour before we were about to go to bed and we were just talking then I asked him if I could go to sleep because the next day we had to get up early as there were some activities planned for the work. It was a double bed, and I was sleeping at the other side, and he was sleeping at the other side of the bed. In the middle of the night, I could feel this guy right behind me. So it is a big bed, and I am sleeping at the other side and could feel that this guy was right behind my back and he is a married guy with a kid. If I would have tried to move a little further, then I would have fallen from the bed. I did not know what to do. I really didn't know at that time. I was just waiting for morning to come and kept thinking about avoiding this situation.* A gay man

Derogatory remarks, non-verbal, physical discrimination and sexual harassment, are not only passed by heterosexual individuals in the workplace but at times there is discrimination within the workplace by some individuals of the queer community towards other individuals from the community. For instance, we have also observed instances where gay men in the organisation have passed derogatory remarks for bisexual, transgender, lesbian women or even other feminine gay men in the same organisation. Though most of these instances that we observed during our research were verbal or non-verbal in nature, there were a few instances where individuals from the queer community verbally, non-verbally and physically discriminated towards other members of the community.

> *Many times it would happen that at office party they (other individuals from the community) try to dominate you. Even if I am a trans-man you have no right to touch me. People make this excuse that I am touching you like a boy, but I can sense that you are not touching me as you would touch a guy friend. My body can sense the intention behind a person touching me. So even gay men for that matter they will also not be sensitive. They think that trans-men do not have problems with random people touching and feeling them but we do have a problem.* A transgender man

Though our sample size is not large enough to validate it to the larger community, over the period of research and our interaction with the community, we have noted that there is discrimination within the LGBTQ community. Individuals from the LGBTQ community who are not out in their organisation have also reported passing sexist remarks to confirm with the heteronormative culture mainly with the intention of protecting their own identity. Other transgender individuals participating in the research had experienced instances of sexual harassment within the community. According to most of them when they disclosed their identity of a transgender individual, people including individuals from the LGB community become curious with regard to what is inside their pants! This is a result of power and privilege positions that one individual or group has over another individual or group along with sexual tension and lack of knowledge as a result of limited interaction and communication due to the cultural sanction of gender behaviour with people from different gender categories.

Fear of Discrimination

For almost all the individuals who were closeted or had disclosed their gender and sexual orientation identity to only a few close people at their workplace informally, their main reason for not coming out was the fear of discrimination and prejudice that their colleagues and employers will form for them just based on their non-normative gender and/or sexual orientation identity. As we have seen already from the instances that one of the main reasons for the individuals to not report instances related to discrimination at their workplace was due to the belief system that was reporting will not solve the problem but only increase it further. Most of the individuals who were seeking employment opportunity or were planning to change their organisation due to adverse experience faced at their previous organisation were very cautious with regard to providing any information to the new employers that directly or indirectly would signal their non-normative gender identity and/or sexual orientation. Many of our participants recorded that they had faced a loss of opportunity due to their non-normative gender identity and sexual orientation, but never did their organisation directly cite their gender identity or sexual orientation as a reason. Even in the case of the transsexual man who had gone into depression, the job profile and working condition for him was degraded in an attempt to make the work environment worst for him with an intention that he would quit the job. The organisation was not only successful in achieving this goal but in the process did harm the individual so much that the individual suffered from chronic depression. Even after he recovered from the depression which took three years, he doubted not only his ability to perform but also his ability to successfully foster long-term engagement with one organisation.

It has been very rare that an individual from the community has reported to not have witnessed any form of discrimination at the workplace or during the selection process. There was one participant who is out in all the spaces, reported that he had never faced any loss of opportunity due to his non-normative sexual orientation in his entire career. Though many organisations had rejected him due to his non-normative sexual orientation, he does not consider it a loss of any opportunity as it was never an "opportunity" according to him if the organisation is intolerant of recruiting individuals from the LGBTQ community. Thus, this individual considered only equal employment opportunity as "opportunity" and organisations that were biased were never seen as an opportunity. To ensure the same, this individual would always reveal his identity of a gay man in the interview process itself and also attempted confirming with the officials if the organisation believed in equal employment opportunity. This did not mean that he did not face any discrimination in these organisations that had considered him for the role despite his non-normative sexual orientation identity, but the individual was assured that he would be able to report instances of discrimination as he did not have anything to hide. We have to remember that every individual from the community has their own process of coming out and that various factors influence coming out the process for each individual. Not everyone can come out and disclose their non-normative gender and sexual orientation identity in their organisation.

Organisations which give employment to people from the community discriminate in giving promotions, appraisal and feedback when they come to know that the person belongs to the queer community. The fear of discrimination was present not only at the entry or operational level of the organisation but also with individuals who were closeted at the leadership position. Interestingly, some of the individuals at the operational level felt that it was easier to come out at a senior level due to the power and autonomy that they would have in the organisation. At the same time, closeted individuals in leadership positions felt that they had far too much to lose by disclosing their identity as a senior employee of the organisation. Further, they also feared that they would not be respected as a leader in their organisation and that the organisation might even attract negative branding if they came out and disclosed their identity at a senior level. According to these individuals at the higher positions, one should come out at the beginning of their career to avoid complications later when they would have more responsibility. There were only a handful of individuals who were out at their workplace and did not fear losing their job. These individuals were out in most of the spaces of the society, for instance, to their family and friends. The general perception of individuals who were out in their work along with other personal spaces such as to family and friends was that the perceived fear of discrimination and harm due to disclosure of their identity was much higher as compared to when they actually come out.

Managing Information Related to Non-Normative Identity and Coming Out

Dr Evelyn Hooker first coined the term "coming out" in the 1950s. According to Dr Hooker, coming out is the process when any person believes themselves to be homosexuals and struggles to identify with this identity in public spaces. Often in the past, homosexuals would visit the "gay" bars due to lack of physical and virtual meeting spaces and signal their sexual orientation to not only the heteronormative society but also other gay/queer individuals in these bars. Public acknowledgement, self-acceptance and the role of gay bars in the form of promoting safe spaces for the queer community, especially gay men, have been associated with the process of coming out. But the context in which coming out has been used since the 1950s has changed a lot. When in the 1950s, coming out signified communal solidarity and hope for the queer community, by 1970s it signified isolation, loneliness, self-hatred and the closet. Today, as Ash Beckham (2013) puts it, coming out can also mean having a hard conversation which does not necessarily have to be related to the LGBTIQ community. It could be any conversation that an individual finds difficult to communicate to other individuals. In this book, we have associated coming out with disclosure of non-normative gender and sexual orientation identity by the LGBTQ individuals.

Individuals from the community first have to come out to themselves which means acceptance of their queer identity to the self. Once the individual has accepted that they identify as queer or with the LGBT community, the process of disclosure or non-disclosure of their identity to other individuals or groups begins. Most of the participants that we interviewed for this book expressed that they were aware of their sexual orientation from a very young age, but accepting the same as part of their identity has been a difficult process. Initially, these individuals had tried to deny their queer identity, but after a point, they felt it was difficult to run away from the "truth." For most individuals who are in the closet, concealing this truth/reality has become their truth!

Coming out for most of the individuals is not a single event. For most, it is a continuous never-ending process. Further, it is to be noted that it is not necessary that an individual may be out or coming out in a similar fashion in all the spaces. Some of the participants also expressed that it is not necessary that every queer individual has to come out to everyone in society. At the same time, a few felt that it was necessary to come out due to their belief system that "personal is political" and that unless enough individuals talked about their sexuality and gender, the society would never be sensitised. However, even these individuals agreed that though they have reached a level where they are comfortable talking about their non-normative gender and/or sexual orientation identity, communication around this issue had not always been so easy with them facing difficulties at some or the other point in the initial phases of coming out. At times even today, these individuals face difficulties while communicating their gender and sexual orientation identity in some spaces or to some groups and individuals. During the research, it was observed that people who were out in the larger spectrum of society were respected more within the community as compared to people who were closeted to the society, but out to just a few individuals from the community. All the participants, even those who were closeted to the mainstream society, said that they were out to at least a few people within the queer community and this is also one of the reasons why we have been able to interview these individuals. It becomes extremely difficult to capture individuals who are not out in any space for the research, and thus, this book is the representative of the voices of only self-identified individuals from the community. Technology has also enabled individuals to live a part of the identity that they may not have been able to live in the "real" world. We have discussed in detail how technology has impacted the lives of the people from the community in Chap. 4.

Overall, non-disclosure of identity has been due to the fear of rejection, ignorance and isolation from the society which had further been strengthened due to the re-criminalization of Section 377 after December 2013. Many individuals who had come out after the High Court verdict started going back into the closet because of reinstatement of Section 377 by the Supreme Court. Interestingly there was a small section of people who started coming out to display their non-acceptance and rejection of the Supreme Court's verdict on Section 377 of the IPC. But these individuals were individuals who were already out in some of the spaces and found support systems in at least some of these spaces. The law and legal status of individuals in their country for identifying with the LGBTQIA community plays a vital role in either disclosure and/or non-disclosure of their non-normative identities in the society. This became strongly evident when we were able to meet and identify more individuals from the transgender community after the NALSA verdict. The ease with which we could find individuals for our research from diverse backgrounds after the NALSA verdict which legalised the status of the third gender as a gender category was a major indication signalling that legitimisation of status and identities in the society becomes an essential factor in determining the closet status of people from the LGBTQ community.

The best way to reach people from the community was by attending formal and informal meetings organised by groups working with the LGBTIQ community. Most of these groups were informal in nature which would plan their meeting through social media. Most of the people who attended the meetings were closeted to most sections of the society and came to the meetings as they felt that this was the only space where they could express their true selves. After interacting with the organisers of this group, we came to know that it is easier for people to come out in queer groups, as closeted people shared similar problems related to their identity in the personal and professional spheres of life. Older members who had been part of such groups were out to everyone or most of the people attending in the group, but the new members at times initially used pseudo names to introduce themselves. Initially, the new member comes to the meeting with the intention of seeing what is happening in such meetings, if they relate with the people and the activities conducted by these groups. Once they attend a few meetings and feel comfortable, they would come out to a few of the members of the group and eventually to the whole group (most people in the group). Interestingly, the process of coming out for individuals in these groups was not very different from the process of coming out in other spaces. However most people eventually came out to the group as compared to other spaces.

We also attended the pride march and events conducting during the pride month in cities like Mumbai and Hyderabad. We noted that not everyone attending the pride march or events would identify with the community and there would be individuals/groups that would participate as allies to the community. Further, we also noted that interestingly most of the individuals who identified with the community and attended the pride march were out at least in some of the spaces or informal groups from the LGBTQ community. Recently, I was having a conversation with one of the individuals who identified as a gay man and asked him if he would be attending the pride march this year. To which he responded

> *Are you mad! I have never attended the pride march. It is so risky there especially with all the police force and the right-wing government, and you never know what will happen. I am the only child and the sole livelihood provider to my parents. I cannot afford to take such risk.*

The fear of not coming out in public spaces even when there is a representation by other out LGBTQ individuals is due to fear of stigma and structural suppression. This is also one of the prominent reasons resulting in limited or non-reporting of the discriminatory instances in most spaces including their workplace. Though individuals who were not out in the workplace felt that having other individuals from the community out in their workplace will help them assess the situation and the homophobic/transphobic climate. Further, the closeted individuals also connect with those who are out formally or informally to have a glimpse and understanding of the world that one experiences when they are out.

Majority of the participants who were out only to some of the colleagues in their organisation reported the main reason they were facing identity crisis at their workplace was due to difficulty in managing the flow of information with colleagues who knew their sexual orientation and colleagues who did not have any idea about their sexual orientation. They had to always be cautious about what they were speaking and how they were acting in front of the colleagues, especially while interacting with those who did not know about their sexual orientation. The primary concern was the fact that if the information was not managed properly by them then it would have an impact on their career. A gay participant who is out and working in an organisation which had an inclusive and diversity policy for the LGBTQ employees reports that despite the policy, employees belonging to the community do not want to come out to everyone because of the fear that coming out would affect their career growth and prospects in the organisation. Further, the spillover effects of coming out may also affect other spheres of closeted employee's life. Thus, some individuals strictly believe in keeping their personal and professional lives separate even when they struggle to do the same. They do not share and/or avoid sharing any information that may hint at their sexual orientation and/or gender identity in the workplace.

Yes, and they are my friends, and I have one sitting across me, and two of them sit in other offices, and I connected with them because of our common sexual orientation. Some people have come out, and some are still scared. They are out within the group. So there are groups of people like me...lest bother and 'let's be ourselves and meet in the cafeteria' and then there are certain groups of people whom we know as part of the community but they are like 'okay...I will chat online on WhatsApp...but I do not want you to meet and all.' So they are not as comfortable. So everyone has their own transition time...some are comfortable or some just want to have sex or some are just okay with their sexuality and some want to at least behave normal. We Indian's are breaded in such a way that we do think that your career is the most important. We have to reach at some point. Earn money but we are not taught to be good human beings...maybe we want to live a lie. A gay man

Strategies to Come Out

Depending on various factors, an individual decides to come out. Disclosure of identity should not be understood in the form of a binary which means that considering that a person can be either out or not. The individual may be partially out and/or hinting at their sexual orientation, but may not directly declare that they identify with the LGBTQ community. Further, the individual may be formally out or informally out. When an individual is formally out, they declare their non-normative gender and/or sexual orientation identity in formal proceedings. For instance, an individual may come out during the interview process or while applying to the organisation. They may even come out formally later after joining and, at times, even while leaving the organisation by informing appropriate authorities about their identity. Most of the time, formal disclosure is clearly communicated where the interpretation of the message does not have room for assumptions. We observed that in the Indian context more number of people come out informally at their workplace rather than coming out formally. Again, various factors play to this informal coming out, but three significant factors that refrain the individual from not coming out formally are

1. The individual does not feel that the organisational climate is safe for coming out. There are no rules or protocol to handle discriminatory issues related to non-normative sexual orientation and gender identity. Also, many individuals believe that unless there are safer laws that protect the rights of individuals identifying with the LGBTQ community on a national level, it is not safe to disclose identity even

in organisations that are LGBTQ-friendly and promote inclusion and diversity of the community within the organisation. Now that the law has changed and homosexuality is decriminalised, it would be interesting to see how it would impact the coming out of individuals especially those who refrained to come out primarily due to the law.
2. The individual is deprived of benefits that heterosexual married employees get for their partners. Even when the person comes out, the person from the queer community will not get these facilities in most of the organisations as there is are no obligatory legal compliance that organisations need to take care since same-sex marriage is not recognised in India yet. Along with this, there would be fear of loss of professional growth opportunity as a result of bias that other employees and employer would have with regard to non-normative gender and sexual orientation identities.
3. There is also a fear of spillover effect especially for employees who are not out to their family and their organisation, and the family is located in the same city.

Overall, individuals who do not want to disclose their identity pass the questions that might hint towards their non-normative gender and sexual orientation identity. Most of the time, the questions that are asked are not direct questions about the individual's sexual orientation and gender identity. They are mostly generic, and indirect questions such as "When are you getting married?" or "What did you do on the weekend?" and other such questions related to the daily life of the individual. An individual who has not disclosed their identity and is dating another person from the same gender may not be able to respond to such questions with answers such as "I went for a movie with my same-sex partner" or "I cannot get married to the person whom I love as I am gay!" It has been noted that if an individual avoids these generic questions for a long time, then it might ultimately lead to a disconnect with their colleagues as they would not be able to develop a bond due to lack of sharing intimate and personal information which is very typical in the Indian workplace.

Another way of not revealing the non-normative gender and sexual orientation identity is by providing false information that would help them project the heteronormative identity. For instance, a gay man may talk about "how he finds a woman in the office attractive" with other male colleagues to project himself as being heterosexual. While this strategy helps the individuals to connect with other colleagues, the premises of this bond is built on false information, and it often harms the individual in the long run. Most of the people who were using fabrication as a strategy and had spent considerable time in the organisation reported that they faced difficulty remembering all the false information which often leads to confusion amongst them and their colleagues. Often individuals using this strategy have also experienced identity crises due to their inability to manage multiple false identities. Few individuals also used concealment as a strategy where they would take preventive, proactive steps that people at their workplace would not question and discover their non-normative gender identity and/or sexual orientation. This strategy was mostly used by individuals who had past negative experiences due to disclosure of their identity. People may use one or more strategies at the same time for concealing their identity. For instance, a person from the community may be using fabrication and concealment together as a strategy to prevent their identity from getting disclosed. Also, the individual may use a different strategy with different sets of people in the workplace. We noted that individuals who did not want to come out preferred "passing" as a strategy while interacting with their boss or people in higher authority. This is mainly due to the paternalistic nature and limited two-way interaction of individuals with their superiors at the workplace. The strategies might differ for individuals who want to hide their identity from their immediate supervisor, as the relationship and the bond shared with the immediate supervisor may not be as unidimensional as compared to other leaders in the top management level. While concealing their identity with their subordinates and colleagues, most individuals preferred using fabrication and/or concealment as a strategy to protect their identity.

Many individuals also came out and disclosed their identity in interesting ways. Most of the people who came out by choice in their workplace were out in some other space as well and had prior exposure with regard to the reactions of people and subsequent post-disclosure impact. In most of the cases, individuals came out first by signalling or giving a cue about their identity to colleagues they trusted most. This was followed with their attempts to normalise their identity in comparison with that of the heterosexual identity. Often, individuals attempted to normalise their identity by arguing that just because their sexual orientation or gender identity was not normative, does not mean that they do things differently compared to that of cis-gender heterosexual people. Normalising became an essential strategy in the process of coming out, as a large part of the Indian society still considers identities that do not fit in the traditional gender model as "abnormal." Some of these individuals also reported having faced exhaustion and a sense of burn-out due to constantly being in a position where they had to educate and answer the questions of people all the time. As a result of which some also stopped normalising and just disclosed their identity which was in most cases direct communication about their non-normative gender and sexual orientation unlike signalling.

There were also a few individuals who were out in most of the spaces and freely talked about their lives with an identity that is considered non-normative. Further, some of these individuals had also come out formally to their organisation, but the representation of such individuals who were out and proud in their workplaces was rare. No wonder that Indian LGBTQ youth do not have enough role models in their workplace. A difference was noticed with regard to the coming out strategy in individuals who were partially out or where in the process of coming out in most of the spaces compared to that of people who were already out in most of the spaces by choice. For individuals who were partially out or wanted to come out, the communication was around justifying and normalising their non-normative gender and/or sexual orientation identity. At the same time, in the case of individuals who were already out by choice, their communication was around celebrating the differences that people have in a society even when they are different. Both the groups had a desire to be accepted, but one wanted to be accepted on the grounds of similarities whereas the other wanted to be accepted on the grounds of the celebration of diversity.

The Impact of Discrimination

The impact of discrimination has differed from individuals depending on various factors some of which are their closet status, position in the organisation, and support system within and outside the organisation. Some respondents who were discriminated at their workplace thought that they could have been more productive in the organisation if they had received formal support from their organisation with regard to inclusion practices. Some individuals faced difficulty in connecting with other employees and colleagues informally as they could not share details about their personal lives. Not being able to maintain real connections with colleagues at the workplace also changed the group dynamics and the role that these individuals played in their organisation. Majority of the respondents who were out only to some of the colleagues in their organisation reported the main reason they were facing identity crisis at their workplace was due to difficulty in managing the flow of information with colleagues who knew their sexual orientation and/or gender identity as compared to colleagues who did not have any idea about their sexual orientation. They had to always be cautious about what they were speaking and how they were acting in front of the colleagues who did not know about their sexual orientation. The primary concerns with these respondents were that if the information were not appropriately managed by them then it would have an impact on their career negatively. Few even lied about their relationship status to their colleagues at the workplace. Some individuals were clear about not coming out even informally to any employees in the organisation due to the spillover effect of coming out. It has to be noted that even if an organisation has policies for the inclusion and diversity of the LGBTQ employees, it is not necessary that all the employees belonging to the community would come out in the organisation.

Transgender and transsexual employees were more vulnerable to discrimination and reported the highest degree of identity crises. Two transsexuals, one who had started consumption of hormones and another who had not started the process of transformation, reported that they were asked to confirm with their biological gender rather than the gender they identified with, till they had completed the process of transformation. One of the transsexual men underwent identity crises only till the point he was unable to complete the transformation process. He reported that he did not feel any crises related to his identity once the process of transformation was completed. He felt "himself" in his body, and thus transformation in itself was the biggest reason for the end of his identity crises. This was also reported by some of the gay participants who were out in their organisation. For these gay participants coming out of the closet had empowered them and helped them overcome the identity crises when they were in the closet. They felt liberated and authentic to themselves when they came out of the closet. For these transsexual and gay individuals, identity crisis was mostly internal and related to the ability and freedom of expression with regard to their sexual orientation and/or gender identity. Thus, these individuals valued acceptance of self-identity more compared to non-acceptance of their identity by other individuals. Identity created by the self, overpowered the construction of identity which was expected and accepted in the society. Further, for these participants, acceptance of the true self became more critical than exclusion and discrimination that they would have to face due to such expression which challenged the heteronormative society at large. A few gay participants were out in the open and felt that they did not face any identity crises because they did not have to pretend to be someone else for which the society would accept them.

It is to be noted that here identity crisis occurs due to the gap between how participants perceived themselves and what they want to be perceived as or the gap between how they want others to perceive them with respect to the way others perceive them.

> *Every second, every minute, every day and every month not only at the workplace, everywhere—other than the time I am spending with the Queer Campus (an informal LGBTQ support group) meeting that is the only time I do not have any crises. I am open but otherwise, it is like I am wearing a mask a very ugly mask which is difficult to fit my face but still I am bearing with it.*

IDENTITY CRISES

Individuals who are not out or partially out only to a few people in their organisation have reported facing identity crises while managing information with their non-normative gender and sexual orientation identity. In India, it is prevalent to have personal conversations related to family and partner at the workplace. For instance, one of the organisations that we were working with had days where employees could invite their family members or partners at the workplace as a diversity and inclusion practices. The broader intention for this activity was that the employees develop a bond with their colleagues on a personal level as well as take pride in their workplace along with their contribution to the organisation. These types of events and activities are very heteronormative by nature as they do not provide an opportunity of expression for the individuals with non-normative gender and sexual orientation especially to those who are closeted in their organisation.

We have already seen that even a simple conversation like "What did you do on the weekend?" may lead to an indication of the sexual orientation of an individual. For a heterosexual individual, it might be effortless to respond to this question that they spend this weekend with their partner, but the same may not be possible for the LGBT employees who are not out and at times even out but have not disclosed their relationship which is not normative as it was also against the law of the land till 2018.

While it is not a crime to identify with the LGB community, it is a crime for individuals from the non-normative gender and sexual orientation to be in a sexual relationship which is not peno-vaginal. Thus, even an individual who is out in their organisation may feel restrained while providing any information related to their partners due to the fear of the law. Saying that they are in a relationship or are even using various platforms to meet other queer individuals will also imply and be assumed that the relationship is sexual in nature.

Acceptance of the true self became more critical than exclusion and discrimination that they would have to face due to such expression which challenged the heteronormativity in the society at large. One of the gay respondents, who was out in the open, felt that he did not face any identity crises because he did not have to pretend to be someone else for which the society would accept him. He said:

> *I would hate to be called straight…I would not want to be 'too' straight because I would consider that to be quite an insult because I think that being gay…it is my sexuality, so why should I be like someone else? So if my boss tries to make me 'too' straight, then I am not happy with it…I am happy being gay but I am not happy being 'too' straight because…even if I am 'too' gay it is my sexuality, to be heterosexual which is what being deviant for me…for me being homosexual is being in my skin.*

The process of disclosure and non-disclosure changes depending on various factors. Though primarily coming out is communication around non-normative gender and sexual orientation identities that individuals have, each event is different from the previous with regard to the way this information is communicated and the way people/group that the individual is coming out reacts to this information.

Living in Fear

Individuals from the LGBTQ community who have not revealed their identity at the workplace have consistently reported being living in fear. Various strategies are used by individuals to manage information related to their non-normative gender and/or sexual orientation at the workplace.

Most of the respondents who were closeted did not want to come out because they feared losing their job and being isolated from society. A physiotherapist who was not out to anyone but only to the community said:

Actually I am scared that if anybody comes to know about this, then I will be in grievous condition...my career would be lost...and suppose my male clients come to know that I am gay then obviously they will not allow me to do therapy with them. Particularly the therapy which involves touching patients. Sometimes you have to lift them up...you have to carry them...you know you have to make them do the exercises...so honestly...I am a gay person and I have libido but I can very honestly say that from the bottom of my heart and conscious that whenever I touch the patient, never did I see him from any other point of view other that a patient...but will they understand if I tell them...will they understand my honesty...they will not understand and even my employer may not understand...he is also a physiotherapist...a professor but still he will not understand. So that is the reason I am not coming out in my organisation. Suppose I come out my career would be zero. The fear of losing everything...everything (emphases on everything)...everything in my vocation.

COURTESY STIGMA

The stigma attached to those who associate with the stigmatised is known as the courtesy stigma. In the narration below, we can see that a physiotherapist was stigmatised for treating transgender patients. The physiotherapist identified as gay but was not out to anyone in his organisation.

At one instance, we happened to attend a transgender case...first time it was done...and you know the senior of our hospital had some other work and she asked me to take care of the patient. I met and attended the patient and did the subsequent follow up. Also, that person used to come to me because I used to be very friendly and caring, so you know my colleagues started booing me...you know they started saying that 'you are a specialist for these people.' So I do not know why... they said that there must be a similarity between you and them, and that is they are coming to you and like that, I faced some kind of discrimination. But I did not give any importance to that and I continued with my service. And it so happened that this patient started to bring all this kind of patients to me from his community. And then you know I really...let me give my confession on this record...I didn't want to do it but I had to tell him that 'Why are you coming only to me. There are too many people that are working here.' I am facing a lot of problems because you people are coming only to me...so please go to other doctors...I should not have told them this. I mean the code of medical ethics does not allow us to say that...I mean we cannot reject or say no to a patient...but you know...because of this discrimination...I had to tell them to go to another physiotherapist.

From the above narration, we can also see how the colleagues of this respondent "othered" transgender people when they say that "you are specialist for these people." At the end of the narration, we can see that due to the fear of being "othered" and being discriminated the respondent does not want to associate with the transgender people. It becomes important for him to manage his heterosexual identity in front of his colleagues to avoid discrimination. This is a classic case when even though the individual identifies with the LGBTQ community, they do not want to associate with other individuals who are out or visibly queer in their workplace due to the fear of association ultimately leading to discrimination. We have already seen that it is prevalent for individuals from the community to face indifferent behaviour from their colleagues. One of the primary reasons is fear of courtesy stigma which may result in discrimination and loss of growth opportunity at the workplace.

Coping Mechanism

Most of our participants have reported facing one or more instances of discrimination and/or indifferent behaviour in their organisation.

Irrespective of the closet status, we have seen a similarity with respect to the stereotypes and comments that individuals across India face in their organisation with regard to their non-normative gender identity and sexual orientation. It was noticed that these stereotypes and derogatory remarks to describe them were also similar, but the way these individuals reacted to the comments was different. Most of the time, individuals who were out either did not bother about such comments or confronted the person who was passing such comments on them. At the same time, individuals who were closeted in the organisation did not react at all to such comments. They became more emotional while talking about such discriminatory instances during the interview, whereas individuals who were out felt that they had got used to such comments and took a decision of confronting or not confronting the person depending on the formal and informal relationship they shared with this person and, at times, even groups. Most of the individuals who were closeted or only out to few people in the organisation had to face such derogatory comments mostly because they were visible as queer in some or the other way. The partially out respondents rarely confronted the person who was passing such comments. This was not an issue faced by closeted cis-gender queer individuals. The individuals going through such instances of discrimination felt that they would invite more trouble due to non-acceptance of non-normative gender identity and sexual orientation by a majority of the Indian society. Further, most of the individuals at the operational level or who were just beginning their career also did not react to such instances as a result of shock and confusion resulting from these instances. Individuals who were at the early stage of their career and were not able to cope with the discrimination at their workplace either ended up quitting their job or were seeking another employment opportunity. Further, these individuals, even reported facing discrimination in other spaces of the society; but they were not prepared for or had rarely imagined that they would encounter any such instance in their workplace. This was mainly due to the belief system of corporate spaces being professional and formal along with the belief that their sexuality or gender identity did not/should not matter at their work. Individuals who were discriminated against at their workplace had a change of perception with regard to their non-normative gender identity and/or sexual orientation impacting their work and their life. They realised that it was difficult to conceal their gender identity and/or sexual orientation at their workplace where they were spending most of their productive time in a day and interacting not only formally but also informally with various individuals. Closeted cisgender individuals who were at the early stage of their career and had not faced any instance of discrimination directly continued believing that their sexual orientation should not be discussed or disclosed at their workplace as it strictly comes under their private life which had no reason to be mixed with their professional life, thus marking a clear segregation between their personal and professional life. Individuals who came out accidentally did not react to the discriminations and derogatory comments as they were mentally not yet ready to come out.

> *There are two people in my organisation who are out of the closet, but there are people who are a little frenzy. They pass comments like 'see he is walking like a girl'—that is discrimination. People who are out they often don't face much discrimination, and even if they do they develop a thick skin by then that they do not call it an instance of discrimination…like for me if someone calls me guud (faggot), I will confront that person 'Yes, I am. So?' I will not even take it as discrimination. That's me, but a new person who walks into my office and is bullied would he feel discriminated? I would say that my office is discriminatory at a certain level. There is still no safe haven for LGBT people.* A gay man

One might get confused as to what is then discrimination for the community because a few of them feel that they have been discriminated, while the others from the community feel that it was not discrimination for them as they are "used to" such comments and it does not affect them emotionally. Some people from the community would have not at all reacted to such derogatory comments. While deciding what discrimination is and what it is not, the intention and impact of the instance have to be taken into consideration. Also, just because an individual is not responding to such instances does not mean that they are not being discriminated. This resonates very much with the issue of domestic violence in our society where outsiders are confused if the person abused should be supported with help as it is there "personal" matter.

It is true that the people who have been affected by such derogatory comments and actions should decide for themselves if they have been discriminated. Even when an individual feels that they are being discriminated they may not be able to report or share the same due to various reasons such as the fear that it will be revealing their own identity which is considered not normative, not having any policies and infrastructure to address these issues and fearing further discrimination. In case such an issue is reported in an organisation then we must remember that the issue here is that of discrimination and not that of knowing if the person who is being discriminated has a non-normative gender and sexual orientation identity. Ultimately, the individual determines what accounts for discrimination, but we can still have guidelines with respects to the type of language and behaviour that is acceptable in the organisation for any stakeholder irrespective of their gender or sexual orientation identity.

A queer individual who is out in open said:

Now if my friends tell me that (name) faggot, you come here...do I take that as bullying? Bullying is when I tell that it is bullying, bullying is not when you see it is bullying. Certain people are okay and if you as an activist would get offended when people are talking to me like that's too bad for you. It is not what you think, it is what I define. A queer individual

People from the community reported during the interview that straight people always talk either directly or indirectly about their sexuality in the workplace. When heterosexual individuals talk about their marriage, their girlfriend, relationship and their in-laws, they are also revealing their heteronormative identity, but many individuals from the queer community even find these conversations difficult as they may hint towards their non-normative gender and/or sexual orientation identity. The respondents felt that it was only because society recognised the heterosexual relationship and marriage under the traditional gender model as a valid and moral institution. Homosexuals in such a society would not get the fundamental human rights of loving, marrying or spending time with the person that they want to and the ability to express themselves honestly in everyday conversations.

Most of the individuals identifying with LGBTQ identities felt that the community had played a significant role in helping them to get through bad times and being/providing a support system when there was none. Further, these individuals felt that people from the community could understand the problem that they have faced because they have or are already witnessed/witnessing similar kind of problem and discrimination in their lives too. Most of the closeted individuals who did not feel close and confident enough to their family to discuss about their problems and the thoughts related to their gender identity and sexual orientation turned for help to the community. Some individuals also felt that they had found an extended family in the community. All individuals interviewed for this book have been part of some informal queer community/group in their city. Individuals from the metropolitan city had multiple options of informal and formal queer and LGBT groups that they could associate with. Various factors such as proximity, ideologies of these groups, nature of the group and type of events that the group would organise became the reasons for individuals from the community choosing to associate with a particular or multiple groups. While in the non-metro cities, there was a lack of existence of such groups and if any group for LGBTQ individuals existed they were majorly informal in nature. Though individuals from both metro and non-metro cities had access to virtual groups, the awareness for different types of virtual groups was more amongst the individuals from metropolitan cities. The individuals from the non-metro cities witnessed lack and desire for community support to the extent that some individuals had acquired jobs or desired to be employed in metropolitan cities so that they could meet and interact with more people belonging to the community. Similarly, many individuals from the community who were settled in the city expressed a desire to migrate to countries that had equal rights for the LGBTQ community. The common thing irrespective of the geographical location of these queer individuals was that each desired to be in a better, open, understanding and inclusive environment so that they could have a better life.

Unfortunately, there were no formal support groups in most of the organisations. Even most organisation which has an inclusive policy for the LGBT community did not have formal support groups within the organisation for the LGBTQ individuals, thus, most of the time restraining inclusion of LGBT employees only at the policy level. A closeted gay respondent, who regularly goes to meet his friends from the community on the weekends, felt that the only time he is true to himself and is able to live his real identity is the time when he is with the community. Otherwise, at his workplace and even at home when he is with his parents and relatives, he feels that he has to manage an identity which he does not identify with,

> *I cannot be myself in my company. Really sometimes, whole week I will just wait for Sunday. When I will meet my friends, when I will be myself. The entire week I will just be thinking about them and all my group friends because I can't express myself or cry in front of my colleagues. I cannot share anything with them. I cannot laugh with them. In the company, I will try to be busy with my work. So I will just talk with one or two colleagues. I will not go out with them. But then I would rather prefer to be alone. Even if I have lunch with them, then I will not talk to them (colleagues) during that time.*

Somebody who is from the community and is out as queer also becomes a support system and a gateway to the world which closeted people cannot access yet. Since the person is out and has seen how people have reacted to them, they are in a better position to guide and listen to those who are closeted. An individual who is out, said that he became the source of coping mechanism for two people who were closeted in his organisation.

Interestingly, almost all the respondent said that a person with the same sexual orientation and/or gender identity has played a role in some or the other way to help them cope in difficult times. For instance, it was easier for a transsexual female with another transsexual female, a lesbian with another lesbian and so on. Though as already mentioned, this option may not have been available to individuals from the non-metro cities. An accepting family member and sibling also have helped the respondents to cope up. Many respondents have also reported that information technology and social media has played a significant role not only to cope but also to network with people from the community. For some individuals, it was relatively easier to come out to their siblings or another member of the same generation in their family or the extended family as compared to their parents. Rarely had an individual been to a counsellor or a therapist to seek help to cope with discrimination. This was reported to be due to the lack and inaccessibility of gender-sensitive counsellors and therapists, along with cultural stigma attached with visiting a professional for mental health accompanied with the fear of coming out. Also, most of the time, visiting the counsellor was reported to be forced by the family members on these individuals as a corrective measure. The instances where the individual from the queer community had visited a mental health professional even when they were aware that they should have sought professional help were rare.

Other things like reading, watching movies, yoga, sex, being in a relationship of their choice and pets have also helped some of the respondents to cope during difficult times. Few individuals also gave in to drugs, alcohol and substance abuse. All the transsexual individuals who had completed or were in the process of transformation thought that getting the sexual reassignment surgery (SRS) completed and changing the gender to the gender that they identified with, also helps them to accept themselves more and acted as their primary coping mechanism. Getting the surgery is a lengthy and expensive process. Further, all the transsexuals may not get support from their family. Thus, for transsexual individuals, the primary coping mechanism was internal as their biggest issue was first to complete their transformation followed by all the other issues attached with the rejection of non-normative gender identity in the society. A transsexual man who has undergone surgery responded,

> *I felt low when I was not taking hormones, I was very depressed, very frustrated because I was not getting a way as how to start my process but due to the knowledge (acquired over a period of time) and internet, I got an idea how to take the hormones or how to start the procedure and after starting the hormones I was very happy, very satisfied.*

Sadly, there was no formal support for most individuals at their workplace and even when there was in few organisations, none of these individuals reported to have benefited from it in time of crises. If there has been any role of the workplace in coping mechanism for these individuals, then it has been informal that too mostly with other queer individuals at the workplace who could be approached especially during difficult times.

References

Beckham, Ash. 2013, October 16. Coming Out of Your Closet. *TEDxBoulder.* https://www.youtube.com/watch?v=kSR4xuU07sc. Accessed 17 July 2014.

Burton, H.W., and S. Bairstow. 2013. Countering Heteronormativity: Exploring the Negotiation of Butch Lesbian Identity in the Organisational Setting. *Gender in Management: An International Journal* 28 (6): 359–374.

Ragins, B.R., and C. Wiethoff. 2005. Understanding Heterosexism at Work: The Straight Problem. In *Discrimination at Work: Psychological and Organizational Bases,* ed. R.L. Dipboye and A. Colella, 177–201. Mahwah, NJ: Lawrence Erlbaum Associates.

CHAPTER 3

Heteronormativity in the Workplace

In the context of heteronormativity, the use of the term "closet" draws attention only to the fact that opposite-sex desire and heterosexuality are better as compared to homosexuality (Butler 1993, 1999; Foster 2008; Yep 2003). This act also leads to the assumption that all individuals are straight unless the person declares their desire towards the same sex or is visibly queer. According to Butler, heteronormativity makes the act of identifying heterosexual as unnecessary, as it is considered to be normal, and requires a person from the LGBT community to "come out." According to Crimp (1993: 305), the closet is not a function of homosexuality in our culture but that of presumptive and compulsory heterosexuality. Thus, in a heteronormative culture, the person has to come out to everyone at all times to be publicly identified as one of the LGBT community. Simply put, heterosexuality and the roles and identities associated with it become the norm in the society.

Making sexuality and gender performativity a norm is not just limited to the larger heterosexual society. The same also stands true for the homonormative/transnormative/queernormative culture where it is assumed that everyone in that space is a homosexual/transgender/Queer, unless they declare their identity otherwise. During the course of this research, it was interesting for me to see how my own identity is/was assumed not only by heterosexual individuals but also by the LGBTQ community. When people would come to know about this research, they would often ask me what motivated me to take this research. With this question,

I always felt that people are trying to know if I also belong to the community or they had already assumed that I belonged to the community, but wanted to hear it from me. Initially, I used to find it tough to tell these people the true reason for me to take up this research. The fact that it was difficult to reveal that I am an insider from the community is because heterosexuality is the norm. Disclosing an identity that is not the norm is considered as a deviant identity—an identity of the outlier. Even individuals from the LGBTQ community would often assume my identity to be that of a gay man. What was more interesting for me was to see that it is not just the identity that is assumed, but also the ideology that one would have when they identify with a certain identity were assumed too. We saw that human beings tend "normalising" the way gender is perceived/performed/lived and this normalisation set the norm not only for the mainstream society but also for the part of society that is not considered mainstream—thus even normalising and validating the mainstream in what is not the mainstream. In this chapter, we would be exploring about what happens when heterosexuality is the norm in the workplace and the manner it impacts the lives of the LGBTQ individuals who may or may not be out.

The debate of nature or nurtured: Even when the discussion around sexuality especially non-normative gender identity and sexual orientation identity is tabooed in most part of the Indian society, we felt that people were open and willing to discuss these issues. As researchers, we had perceived a higher resistance and unwillingness amongst most people to discuss these issues before going to the field. While providing gender and sexual orientation training to people, we were surprised that most people were willing to participate in this difficult conversation, but most of the discussion among the heteronormative society that we intended to sensitise revolved around if having an identity or belonging to the LGBTQ community is natural or is/could be nurtured. At times, it was difficult to go beyond these conversations and address the main problem of discrimination and hate crime faced by the LGBTQ community as a result of their non-normative gender and sexual orientation bias. Myths that were often brought up with regard to homosexuality is that, children who have undergone sexual abuse grow up to be homosexuals and/or that the homosexuals are potential paedophiles. The underlying assumption to all of these arguments is that individuals identify as LGBTQ due to "abnormality" either when they were conceived or when exposed to conditions that are not normal during childhood. Gestational neuro-hormonal theory has been widely used in explaining the factors that lead to homosexuality.

According to gestational neuro-hormonal theory, homosexuality is a result of the difference in prenatal hormone levels (Ellis and Ames 1987). The probability of an individual becoming homosexual increases with the extreme (*abnormal*) level of some prenatal hormones. As per this theory, the sexual orientation of a person cannot be learned through socialisation. Learning from socialisation becomes a powerful tool for expression and negotiation of gender identity and sexual orientation, but sexual orientation is determined long before the process of cultural socialisation (Weill 2009). These research and debates are carried out to find out what leads an individual to identify with the LGBTQ reinforces that people identifying with the LGBTQ community are different from the larger society. It is only because the LGBTQ community does not conform to heteronormativity in the society at some levels which marks them to be different from the society. Further, in most of the societies, these differences are perceived as disruptive to the existing heteronormative structures of the society often leading to "corrective measures" and discrimination.

> *My point is let's not even care about if it is a choice or if it is a natural experience. It does not matter you know that when straight people do not worry about it. Was a straight person ever stopped to think what are the origins of my orientation...why am I straight...am I generally straight or did I turn straight because of my dad. So they are not asking the question then why are we asking the question. We are just the way we are.* A gay man

Though members from the LGBTQ community had their own opinion if being LGBTQ was natural or nurtured, but, for most, this question was not relevant. In fact, many individuals were also angry with the thought that when every day the community is subjected to discrimination and hardships, we as a society are still discussing what causes homosexuality. Being from the LGBTQ community may or may not be a choice, but we know that whatever people identify as in the society is a choice which most of the time is enforced by the majority in the society. For instance, being in a closet and not coming out is a choice. Similarly, choosing not to have a sex life when the society taboos your sexuality is a choice. To every person who is out or closeted, practising a life where they choose to deny their natural inclination is a choice. These are some of the choices that people from the community have to make every day so that they can be a part of this mainstream society. Depending on the degree and extent of heteronormativity in a society, some choices are more difficult as compared to others. At times, the presence of heteronormativity in the society is so high that individuals live an identity that they do not identify with. Most people from the community do not come out because of the enormous price attached with choosing to disclose and live a life which is considered non-normative. The price is so high that it does not eventually remain a choice. For instance, in some countries, homosexuality is punishable with the death sentence; individuals from the community do not really have a choice to live the life that they want to live.

Heteronormativity in Organisations

Organisational spaces are no different from the spaces in society with regard to heteronormativity. In fact, we have witnessed that some organisations can be more heteronormative as compared to other spaces in society. This is the case with organisations that are dominated by cis-gender heterosexual men. Even today, when we talk about gender diversity and inclusion in India, it is only with reference to having more women representation in the workplace. Very few organisations aim for making their organisation's culture diverse and accepting, and realise that just having more number of women in the workplace would not make the organisation more diverse or less heteronormative. At some level, all of us are impacted by the existence of heteronormativity in our society and in the workplace, but individuals who do not confirm or do not appear to be confirming are forced to do the same. It is easier for cis-gender individuals from the LGBTQ community to pass as heterosexual and confirm with the norms of heteronormativity, but even individuals who can pass as a heterosexual person having a normative life have reported being going through identity crises. Further, this compulsion of confirming affects not only them but also the people near them and ultimately the larger society.

> *I think I do not have a problem being gay because I do not overtly act feminine.* A gay man

Married or Gay?

In India, marriage is one of the most significant events that take place in a person's life, and all are expected to get married after a certain age. Unmarried people are interrogated more and more as the right age for marriage passes. These questions do not remain restricted only in personal/social spaces. It is very common in India to talk about family and marriage while recruiting and on the job. If the employee was not out and not married then, they had to tackle questions as to why they were not married. A person who is not married after the "right age" has passed is often assumed to have some problem and hence not considered normal. Further, an unmarried woman faces more stigma as compared to an unmarried man. The "right age" of marriage for women is considered to be much less compared to the "right age" of marriage for men in society. Even the legal age of marriage for women is 18 years compared to their male counterpart which is 21 years. Most Indian families fear if their daughter does not get married at the "right age," then it would become difficult for her to marry anyone. Though this cannot be generalised for everyone in our society, it can definitely be said about a large part of our society. For instance, an unmarried woman of 30 years of age would face more discrimination as compared to an unmarried man of 30 years. This interrogation of why a person is not getting married after a certain age does not remain restricted to the family members and relatives but is also asked by colleagues and other employees in the workplace.

In the initial stages while conducting an interview with the queer employees, discussing marriage was not on our agenda. The focus on marriage came up automatically during the interview, especially when we made inquiries on their identity and process of information management and stigma management concerning their sexual preference. All the participants who were not out and not visibly queer were repeatedly asked when they would be getting married and the reason behind not getting married. Employees who were out reported that they were mainly asked about sex and "gay adventures" out of curiosity by other employees they were close to and sometimes even by other random employees who knew about the respondent's queer identity. During the research, we met many individuals who identified as gay and lesbian, but were married to heterosexual partners who were not aware of their non-normative sexual orientation identity. It was observed that marriage became one of the critical questions that people from the community (especially those who were not visibly queer) were asked even in their workplace.

One of the participants married because he thought that it would "cure" the homosexual tendency. Ultimately, he realised that there was no change in his sexual orientation and marriage had failed to suppress his feelings to be in a same-sex relationship. He ended up getting a divorce. Even while filing for divorce he did not have the courage to reveal the real reason for seeking the divorce. In his workplace, where he had been working for the past eight years, his relationship status of a "divorce" was known to most of his colleagues and since he was not out as gay man nor visibly queer, his identity at the workplace remained that of a cis-gender heterosexual man who was divorced. In this case, we can see that the participant did not face any stigma because of three reasons.

1. Being into a marriage worked as a concealment strategy to manage the flow of information related to his non-normative sexual orientation.
2. He was not visibly queer nor out to any other employee in the organisation.
3. In India, the stigma attached to a divorced woman is much higher than that attached to a divorced man.

I was married and divorced, and most of my colleagues know this. So no one will ask me anything related to that. So suppose I tell my colleagues that I am going to Goa for a holiday and if they ask me 'with whom?' Then I tell them 'friends.' Then there is no more pressure to explain yourself. A gay man

Most of the cis-gender men with non-normative gender and sexual orientation identity were frequently asked about their relationship and marriage status from their male and female colleagues. This was not the case with women with non-normative sexual orientation identity that we interacted with as they majorly reported to be asked questions related to relationship and personal life from most of the other female colleagues and from male colleagues with whom they shared a close relationship at the workplace. However, these women have also reported that once they have spent some time in the organisation, most people including men whom they directly haven't interacted with, would know fragments of details related to their relationship and personal life from the other colleagues.

There are groups…one is the male group and other the female group. So all the female group will ask about marriage and if suddenly as a girl you wear something a lot traditional or something they will pinpoint it and will scan you from head to toe and make you awkward and I found men to be only talking about 'why don't you talk little girlish and act little girlish.' That is the only thing they say. A lesbian woman

This is due to the cultural segregation and appropriateness with regard to what type of communication is generally allowed in a large part of Indian society. In the Indian society, it would be considered inappropriate for a male colleague to ask a female colleague about her marriage plans unless they are close or share a comfortable and understanding informal relation at the workplace. Women from the non-normative gender and/or sexual orientation identity have reported that they feel more remorse and stereotypical comments on their face from other cis-gender women who identify as heterosexual. The woman in the above narrative had masculine attributes and was questioned about masculinity by her male colleagues. This is because women who come across as "butch" or are high on masculine attributes are considered to be generally less attractive in the normative Indian society. In our society, ageing women having butch or masculine attributes are not considered or portrayed as attractive or desirable like the older, matured and masculine men thus making them ineligible to be considered for the "desire" and "attraction" of men in the society. This could also be one of the reasons that none of the colleague of this individual "showed interest" in her or asked her about her relationship as they would have assumed her to be single and/or undesirable for themselves or by other men in the society as well.

The woman in the above narrative was initially avoiding questions related to her personal life at her workplace, but later realised that since she is visibly non-conforming with the gender role, avoiding questions would only affirm that she does not identify as heterosexual. Thus, she started fragmenting information and pretended to have interest in men to avoid any uncomfortable situation at her workplace. We also noted that the women participants who were more masculine and visibly queer were asked more about their relationship and personal details from other women colleagues as compared to women who were cis-gender, but had a non-normative identity. Asking questions related to a romantic relationship is an indirect way for heterosexuals (and at times even for individuals from the queer community) to confirm if the sexuality of the visibly queer/non-conforming individuals identify with the normative society or not. Not marrying at an appropriate age can lead to questioning of the sexual orientation of the person in our societal context especially when marriage is almost a compulsion for every individual. Interestingly, even in societies where issues related to sexuality and sexual orientation is not discussed openly or is considered a taboo, the society develops indirect ways that help them discuss these issues. One of the reasons that marriage is such a big deal in Indian society is because as per the normative societal norms, marriage gives approval and legitimacy to the relationship of couples to be in a sexual and romantic relationship with their partners which otherwise is neither discussed nor considered moral. Thus, confining discussion or experiencing the sexuality of individuals within the boundaries of marriage to a large extent. When in most cases the reason for not getting married is asked to an individual who is unmarried, it is an indirect inference that questions the normalcy of the sexuality of that individual followed by the normalcy of physical and mental health. Depending on the intimacy and the power-relation that people share with each other, they may be directly confronted or inquired about their sexual orientation.

> *One of my colleagues' daughter is not getting married. It seems she asked her daughter if she was a lesbian. Her daughter said that she wanted more time for herself (before she got married).* A gay man

In the case of unmarried closeted respondents who did not have a partner from the opposite sex, didn't discuss being in a relationship with their partner to their colleagues, and didn't participate in the sexual objectification of a person from the opposite gender, the probability for them being labelled as homosexual increased.

> *My friends told me that you should have come out way before to us...they had slight doubts because I never had a girlfriend, I never dated anyone and I was single for a quite a long time. So they were wondering as to what is wrong with me.* A gay man

While some of the participants "used" marriage as a passing strategy, others used it as a part of revealing strategy. In the narration below, the respondent has first used discretion strategy for passing the stigma, then, he uses normalising strategy to reveal his sexual orientation. Similarly, other respondents have revealed their identity by using singling, normalising and differentiating strategies in different spheres of life.

> *When I started working, I usually started chit chatting with my colleagues and there was a discussion about marriage and all that, and I told them that 'Let me find a good boy and then I will marry.' Then they knew about it (my sexual orientation).* A gay man

Though legally individuals who identify as homosexuals cannot marry in India, I met an individual who was married to his partner for the last seven years. He was working in an international banking organisation located in Hyderabad whereas his partner was based in Mumbai. He was in a monogamous long-distance relationship with his partner. He felt that though the society would not accept his marriage, he had nothing to prove to the society and that he had married the person whom he loved the most for his happiness. He was not out in his organisation and used passing strategies for tackling any question related to his relationship or marriage. He felt unhappy about the fact that he could not openly announce his union with this partner and that they could not be accepted as any other "normal" married couple in the society. Even when he was in a committed relationship with his partner, he had to pretend to be single, and in some of the spaces, the relationship with his partner was communicated to be that of "best friends."

Individuals who identified as transsexuals and were undergoing the process of transformation were mostly asked questions about the transition process and their biological sex. Questions related to being in an intimate relationship were rarely asked at the workplace due to the assumption that a heterosexual person cannot fall in love with a transgender individual and willingly agree to spend their life with a person who has undergone sexual reassignment surgery. Most individuals who identified as transgender also felt that an individual is fortunate if they can keep their job and be accepted by their employers during the transition.

HETERONORMATIVITY AND BODY LANGUAGE

I think I do not have a problem being gay because I do not overtly act feminine.

All the men who had feminine characteristics or were visibly queer said that they were and had been discriminated due to their body language which was not as per the expected gender role that men were supposed to play in the society. Further, most of these men who were not out in their workplace always contemplated different scenarios and strategies of tackling discrimination and suppressing their non-normative identity. The discrimination for women who did not confirm was reported to be less as compared to that of men, but as already discussed they faced more discriminatory remarks from their female colleagues at their workplace as compared to their male colleagues. For the transgender individuals, the discrimination due to overall non-conformance with the heteronormative structure had often resulted in discrimination. Some of these transgenders who were also visibly queer reported that they had got used to these acts of discrimination and derogatory remarks that they could be least bothered by the same. Further, these trans* individuals chose to perform the gender role and identity that they related and identified with even at the cost of these discriminatory instances.

Here we need to understand that people may confuse the concept of acceptance with that of discrimination. When the lesbian participants reported to feel accepted as the "other," most of the gay and transgender participants non-confirming with the gender role of the normative society felt discriminated. Some of the lesbian participants thought that in Indian society, it could be an advantage for women to have masculine attributes at times. The society which desires a "boy child" instead of "girl child" and which is so patriarchal in nature, having butch attributes may help. A few even felt that their masculine attributes gave them an advantage over their heterosexual cis-gender colleagues in job profiles such as sales that require a certain element of aggression and masculinity. This is not true for all the industries and job profiles. For instance, a butch woman would rarely be accepted for the profile of an air hostess in the aviation industry, and there are various other job profiles where women are expected to be "attractive" and feminine to provide a "pleasant" experience to the customers!

A butch woman jokingly said that being butch makes them less attractive to men, which indirectly reduces room for sexual tension and sexual harassment as for most of the men she does not exist. She felt that because of the way she looked and identified, she was not an "object" of desire for most of the men dominating the organisation and the society. However, she was perceived to be so undesirable by a large section of the society that it did not lead to any punishment or corrective measure in her case. She was neither considered to be rewarded with "men's love" nor considered eligible for punishment or corrective action. Her only punishment was that she was not desirable for most of the men in our society which she considered a blessing in disguise for her. One of the primary reasons that cause rape or sexual harassment is that men who commit these crimes decide to teach a lesson to the women who are "attractive" to conform to the traditional norms of the society. These norms are anything from not going out at night alone to not wearing a dress which might make the men excited! It is not that butch women are entirely safe from desperate men in the society, but depending on the way they perform gender roles and the degree of non-conformance with the traditional gender roles and identities, she would be relatively considered less desirable. But this does not mean that she would be free from facing derogatory remarks and discriminatory comments from heteronormative men and women in the society.

Butch/masculine women may not be punished as severely as feminine men because masculinity in women is seen as coming closer to being a man, whereas in the case of feminine men they were degrading the status of the men and bringing it down to that of the women. Masculinity would mean not just the physical attributes of the individual but also the gender roles in a society which may be considered masculine or feminine. For instance, women who work or are employed may be considered more masculine as compared to women who are homemakers. Similarly, men who are homemakers may be considered feminine for performing a gender role that is majorly supposed to be performed by women. For individuals who are not cis-gender, it is more about conforming to the physical/visible expectations of what is considered to be masculine and/or feminine in a culture. Men who had visible feminine attributes have reported to being exposed to even physical assault along with verbal and non-verbal discrimination in our society and also in their workplace.

The stereotypical image of gay men has been set in the minds of the people. A gay man is someone who has feminine attributes. Even if such person with feminine attributes identifies themselves as straight, they get the identity of a gay man in the Indian society. In this research, we have included only self-identified LGBT individuals and not people who identify as heterosexual but do not conform to the gender roles laid by the heteronormative structures in the society. Many cis-gender gay participants who were not out in their organisation reported that that since they were not out and did not come across as visibly queer, they had not faced discrimination but at the same time have seen their colleagues make fun and pass derogatory remarks on other individuals who were not able to perform gender in a heteronormative manner.

See the thing is that if you say the word 'gay' there is a thought in human mind that this person would be feminine. There are so many guys in my office who are having this kind of body language which is a bit feminine, but they identify as straight. I have seen that people would mock these guys and often pass comments on the way they sit, the way they talk or the manner in which their hands move. A gay man

Not to me because I have not been out to everyone, but people would obviously not think that I am gay and all that whenever people would come across a feminine guy they will obviously make fun of him. In fact, some people came to me... you know one of my colleague and are commenting 'dekh wo kaise chal raha hai!' (look how he's walking) and they comment about this guy...how feminine this guy is looking and making fun of them so I don't know what to say and I told him that that is his personal issue...then they were telling me that you know 'why are you supporting them?' A gay man

Discrimination may not always be due to sexual orientation or gender but is majorly how gender is performed by people, irrespective of their sexual orientation and gender identity. In this response, the words "more straight-acting" points out the performance of a gender role and gender identity by an individual in the society. It is witnessed that men who have effeminate characteristics are labelled as gay even if they identify as straight. This may also hold true for women who have masculine or butch attributes.

A few gay participants were not taken seriously when they came out to people because they did not have any feminine attributes and they fit in the definition of the "complete man." For gay men who have masculine characteristics, it became difficult for people to accept their sexual orientation for the mere reason that they do not seem to be gay.

> *My identity is that of a straight person at work, and people actually think that I am joking when I say that I am gay at my office including my mom. I was working in an insurance company…there was a lady manager who was interested in me but she was behind me for sex…So it was never with a guy in the workplace…nobody has approached me…it was always with women. I told her that I am gay and that I was not interested…she even thought that I am saying this to avoid her.*

Another participant who had feminine attributes was also questioned as to why he behaved like a "girl" or acted like a "girl." The phrase "like a girl" has got a negative notion attached to it. Being like girls in a heteronormative society is considered to be weak, dependent and not capable and strong enough to be performing various tasks. At the same time, the phrase "like a man" or "you are the man" has a positive notion and is associated with being strong, independent and smart. The society has defined the image of a "complete man" and the "desirable woman." Further, it is expected from the people with such attributes to "perform or act the acceptable gender" and not be themselves if they are not confirming with heteronormativity. One of the participants said:

> *People tell me that I behave like a girl. You are a guy right then talk like a proper guy.* A gay man

Individuals from the community who do not have a normative body language or do not conform to the gendered roles of the society are reminded that they or their behaviour is deviant with each comment or remark. Some have even reported that they have become conscious about their body language and have tried to alter the same in a way that they come across as visibly normative. At the same time, for many individuals even though they are aware that they do not conform, they cannot change themselves to conform with the norms of the society as these behaviours are deeply ingrained in them. A few even feel that gender is not a performance for them, as if it would have been a performance then they would have been able to perform it the way the society would have expected them to perform leading to normalcy. At the same time, there are some individuals who choose to "queer" how gender is performed in comparison with the normative society. Overall, we have noticed that being conscious or being reminded all the time about how they are behaving and what others will perceive with this behaviour, especially when an individual from the community is not out in most of the spaces, impacts the individuals' form of gender expression.

> *When you are gay your behaviour are in a certain way. You cannot help it and you cannot pretend to be a straight guy...there are things which people want to hide but cannot hide. There are things that are attached to you. When I was working, I was sent to Bangalore for a work-cum study program. There was certainly a lot of comments that were passed on me. It was very awful. I use to go to the bathroom and cry. You are victimised at that point of time and you just feel bad about it and you feel like crying and at times you do.* A gay man

Heteronormativity and Gender Appropriate Dressing

We have seen that the way organisations ask their employees to behave in a gender appropriate manner. Though there are some organisations that give their employees the freedom to be themselves, a majority of the organisation control what their employees wear, talk and even how they behave and carry themselves. Employees of the organisations represent the organisation in front of various stakeholders, and the majority of the Indian organisations are not yet ready to be identified as an organisation run and managed by queer employees. This can be inferred with the fact that from all the participants we interviewed only four had worked in organisations having inclusive policies for the LGBTQ employees and most of them were subjected to discrimination.

Different sectors across the labour market have dress codes. It is almost universally accepted by the courts and tribunals in the jurisdictions that the requirements as to employees' appearance are a legitimate concern of management (Wedderburn 1995). Management defines the dress code which fits with the organisational culture and the type of business carried on by them. Sometimes the employee gets an identity due to their dress code, and professionals like doctors, lawyers, police and various others, the profession can be easily identified through the dress that the employee is wearing. A great deal of research has been done concerning the importance of creating an identity the public will accept and respect (Hamid 1972; Molloy 1975; Rucker et al. 1981; taken from Lang 1986). Solomon and Schopler (1982; taken from Lang 1986) have shown that as members of a profession reinforce their image with the public, making this profile becomes the standard by which the populace judges the profession. One major component of this public image is attire (Korda 1975; Littrell et al. 1981; taken from Lang 1986).

While deciding on the dress code and attire, the employer has to consider various factors such as the work environment, type of industry, safety of the employee, comfort level of employees wearing the dress, to name a few. Does the employer consider or even give it a thought to make the dress code gender neutral? Throughout history, various cases have been recorded where women employees have raised their voice as they have been discriminated due to their sex and felt that their status had been lowered due to the difference in policies for men and women that organisations have for dress code.

What difficulties would people from the LGBTQ community face for not adhering to the masculine or feminine gendered dress code in their organisation? Will the organisations accept the transition of transsexuals while such a person is employed? Would transvestites or cross-dressers even be allowed inside the gate of an Indian organisation if they are seeking an employment opportunity?

A transsexual man that I had shadowed during the research dressed like "a man" and though he was proud that he had small breasts that could easily go unnoticed using binders, he was disappointed that people would still have confusion about him and his gender. After getting out of depression, which had lasted for three years, due to the discrimination that he had faced in his previous workplace, he was determined to start afresh and find a new job. He often expressed that he got stares while using both, the men and women toilets in public places and thought that he was considered an outsider at both the places. He went to the job interview and even there because he did not dress gender appropriately, he had difficulty explaining his gender identity in the interview and he told us that the focus of the interview shifted from his capabilities, commitments and his suitability for the job to his gender and questions such as why he was the way he was. Though he made it to the final round of one of the interviews, he was not selected for the job opening. When asked if playing a normative gender role would have impacted him in any way to get employment opportunity he said that there would have been a possibility but then again that was not his identity and he would not have been true to himself had he done anything like that. During the research, I came across a transgender person who cross-dressed when at the community meeting or at his home, but at his workplace he dressed like "a man." He wishes that maybe in future with more progressive laws, he will be able to cross-dress at his workplace and also other open spaces in society.

If the employee does not conform to the gender appropriate dress code or the guidelines given by their employer, then this may serve as grounds for the dismissal of the employee. In the famous case of Boychuk v H.J. Symons Holding Ltd, under British Employment Protection (Consolidation) Act 1978, Ms Boychuk was wearing badges such as "Lesbian ignite" which would indicate her sexual orientation. Since she was in contact with the customers and public in the working hours, the employers felt that such a symbol or sign would offend the customers and other employees. She was warned and then fired for wearing such a badge. The court supported the decision of the organisation of firing the "lesbian who ignored the instructions and did not adhere to heteronormativity."

During the research, we came across a similar case. The only difference, in this case, was that the transsexual man had not undergone surgery, but used male-gendered language while interacting even at his workplace. Since the respondent had to deal with suppliers and vendors of the organisation, he was asked to use language appropriate to his gender. In the narration below the respondent talks about his choice to talk the gendered language, which he identified himself with, but did he really have a choice? This incident took place before the NALSA verdict, but it is difficult to say if the situation would have been any different even after the NALSA verdict as the situation of individuals who identify as transgender largely remains the same.

> There was an organisation where my boss was okay with my identity but did not want my clients to know about my identity and asked me not to talk to the client like a man. That time she told me that I understand what you are and I totally respect it but the vendor is getting very confused so I would suggest not using a male-gendered language in front of them. She kept saying this 'with due respect' repetitively, but it's not about that. It is my choice if I want to talk with a male gender language. I would have really liked if she would have told the clients that 'she' talks like that only instead of me telling to change the gender used while communicating to the vendors and clients. She should have told them not to concentrate on my language but the work I am doing for them. But I do not know what went into her mind and she asked me to use female language while communicating with my clients. In English, we do not have this problem…but Hindi as a language is much gendered. A transsexual man

During the research, we interviewed a few participants working in organisations that did not have a formal dress code policy. Even in organisations where there was no formal dress code, and employees could wear clothing that they felt "comfortable" in—organisations had a problem when individuals did not conform with the dress code that was gender appropriate. This only raises questions that when employees have the freedom to wear whatever they feel comfortable in, why do they have to conform to a dressing style that is heteronormative. Why can't organisations with no formal dress code policy have acceptance for cross-dressing? Does this mean that there is no place in such organisations for transvestites and other people from the LGBTQ community who do not conform with the heteronormative dressing? The incident mentioned below took place a day after the NALSA verdict was passed and transgenders were legally given the status of the third gender. Since the NALSA verdict had been passed a day before, a few media organisations wanted to run a story on transgender individuals in India who are out and proud in different spaces. A leading newspaper wanted to cover the story of a transsexual woman at the workplace; she was advised by her senior to "dress" appropriately and as per the gender assigned at birth as she had not completed her transformation rather than the gender that she identified with. It was ironical that at one end, her story was being covered for daring to disclose her identity at her workplace and, at the same time, she was being restricted from being herself in the same space. Even when people and organisations are becoming inclusive and sensitive towards transgenders, they expect individuals with trans* identity to conform to the traditional gender binary.

When the photographer called me from a leading newspaper, he wanted to take my interview and photos of me...like I am on the phone or writing something on the computer at my workplace. So I asked my boss if the photographer come to the office to click my pictures. Then the boss agreed but he said 'Let him come but don't dress up too much.' So I wanted to wear a nice dress and look nice, but I came in normal clothes without makeup. Otherwise, also he tells me to wear sober clothes so I wear unisexual kind of top as I cannot wear proper female clothes. They said that 'Not now...you cannot wear women's clothing.' So I feel bad and think that when I will have my surgery I will start wearing woman's clothes.

Another incident took place with a gay participant who was out in his organisation and the organisation had a "dress to be creative" policy. On wearing an earring, he was criticised by his immediate superior as it made him look gay. The suggestion by his supervisor for not wearing the earring was that though most people in the organisation knew about the sexuality of this person, he should not flaunt it! During the whole process, the superior kept saying that he did not have any problem with his sexuality, but just the fact that he was wearing an earring.

I am in advertising but my boss once said to me that your earrings are too big... no I don't have a problem with your sexuality but I have a problem with the size of your earrings. So I said that you simply mean that you have a problem with my sexuality...if I put one earring or two earrings or I wear a big earring or a small earring should not make any difference. So I do understand that every office could have a code of conduct which could be formals which could be clothing...It could be any kind of code of conduct but if there is no code of conduct or if you have a relaxed code of conduct then you can't put terms over there saying that you cannot have a piercing or not have an earring because that looks too gay. A gay man

Most organisations follow a "don't say, don't tell" policy when it comes to the non-normative gender and sexual orientation of their employees. Employers would have fewer problems with the person from the community who "acts" appropriate to their gender and do not speak verbally or non-verbally through their actions about their sexual orientation or gender identity. In organisations which have a dress code, even when employees from the community follow this dress code they might still get comments and derogatory remarks for not dressing up to be masculine or feminine enough.

> *In my office, it is compulsory for all the girls to wear traditional clothes only…I mean Indian formal…so even when I wear traditional Indian formals, I still get noticed (for not conforming to the expected norms of femininity). I think there should be the flexibility of wearing the clothes that I want to wear or the way I wanted to carry myself.* A lesbian woman

We would not like to give concluding remarks to this chapter, but instead would ask the readers to think about how are they part of the heteronormative structures in our society and have they ever reinforced or were made to follow these structures.

References

Butler, J. 1993. *Bodies That Matter: On the Discursive Limits of "Sex"*. New York: Routledge.

———. 1999. *Gender Trouble*. Routledge.

Crimp, D. 1993. Accommodating Magic. In *Media Spectacles*, ed. M. Garber, J. Matlock, and R. Walkowitz, 254–266. New York: Routledge.

Ellis, L., and M.A. Ames. 1987. Prenatal Neurohormonal Functioning and Sexual Orientation: A Theory of Homosexuality-Heterosexuality. *Psychological Bulletin* 101: 233–258.

Foster, E. 2008. Commitment, Communication, and Contending with Heteronormativity: An Invitation to Greater Reflexivity in Interpersonal Research. *Southern Communication Journal* 73: 84–101.

Lang, R.M. 1986. The Hidden Dress Code. *The Clearing House* 59 (6): 277–279.

Wedderburn, B. (Lord). 1995. Labour Law and Freedom: Further Essays in Labour Law. *Industrial Law Journal* 24 (3).

Weill, C.L. 2009. *Nature's Choice: What Science Reveals About the Biological Origins of Sexual Orientation*. New York: Routledge.

Yep, G.A. 2003. The Violence of Heteronormativity in Communication Studies: Notes on Injury, Healing, and Queer World-Making. *Journal of Homosexuality* 45 (2): 11–59. https://doi.org/10.1300/J082v45n02_02.

CHAPTER 4

Queer, Information Technology and Internet: The Virtual and the Real

Initially, when we started the research for this book, we had not planned to include the impact of technology, internet and social media on the profession/work life of individuals from the LGBTQ community. As the methodology of the research was exploratory in nature, the role of the internet, social media and other technology with regard to its impact on the identity of the LGBTQ community emerged repeatedly. It was then we decided that we will explore more on the way technology and social media is impacting the lives of the people from the community, especially in their workplace. Soon, we were able to understand that there was an overlap and similarity between the impact of technology and presence on social media with that of the identity that people from the community have at the workplace and in other spaces in the society. This was because the use of technology platforms and presence on social media was similar for all the spaces for most, even when the individuals performed a different identity in different spaces. For instance, individuals may not have disclosed their sexual orientation and/or gender identity at the workplace, at the same time may be out in other spaces, but their social media footprints may easily hint at their non-normative identities even in their workplace.

In the year 2011, a regional news channel broadcasted a "sting operation," where they outed more than ten individuals having a profile on the gay networking site called "Planetromeo." The story that was broadcast was around 7 minutes and raised concerns about how "gay culture" is taking over the society. Photographs uploaded on this social networking website kept continuously flashing during this broadcast. Further reporters from this TV channel also pretended to be gay and got in touch via phone with few men who were active on this networking site. Their conversation with the two men which revealed their identity, that is, their name, sexual preference and various other details of where they study or work, was also disclosed during the broadcast. This horrific incident saw protests by human right activists across India. Even though the Standards Authority fined the TV channel and asked them to pay INR 1,00,000 and ordered them to broadcast an apology in prime time for three consecutive days for violating the broadcasting code in reference to nudity, sex and right to privacy, the damage was already done. This is one of the incidents where the presence and performance of the queer identity on the virtual space put individuals from the community in a jeopardising position. But why is that the Indian LGBTQ community failed to see the dangers of performing a queer identity on the virtual space, or is it that most of the individuals thought that there is no difference between the virtual and the real space. If the overlap in the virtual and real spaces was thoroughly thought out then why is it that the community was willing to perform their "real" identity on the virtual space? We will try and find the answers to these questions in this chapter.

People in India are witnessing an exponential increase in the rate of access to the internet, social media and the integration of technology in everyday lives. Presence on social media platforms is no longer restricted to a particular class of the society residing in the metropolitan cities. Further, technology is becoming an integral part of the youth and upcoming generation. Internet is opening the world and has given visibility to various identities in the society and one such identity which has gained visibility is the LGBTQ community. All the participants that we interviewed are self-identified LGBTQ individuals working in either service or manufacturing industry based in an Indian metropolitan city. Though not all our participants were early technology adopters, all of the participants selected for our research had access to the internet and social media. Most of them were actively present on various social networking websites and mobile applications.

Overall, if we had to categorise our participants with regard to how and when they got broader access to the internet and social media, we could broadly say that there would be an emergence of two major categories based on geographic location and co-habitants, that is, people with whom they shared their house.

1. Classification based on the geographic location: Even though all the participants who we have interviewed for the research were residing in the metropolitan cities of India, most of them had been a native of a rural part of India and had shifted to these metropolitan cities for an employment opportunity. These individuals still had roots with at least a few of their family members and relatives staying in the village. During vacation and free time, they would visit their family and relatives in their hometown/village. Some of the family members of these participants also stayed with them in the metropolitan city, but they kept going back to the village. There were a few participants who were born and raised in the city since childhood. The participants who had lived most of their life span in the metropolitan city had early access to the internet and social media, whereas the participants who had migrated to the city for work became more active on the internet and social media after they started staying in the city. It was not that they did not have access to technology at all before coming to the city, but their presence on different types of platforms increased while living in the city. Also, the time spent on the internet and social media platform had increased as their awareness about various platforms designed explicitly for the LGBTQ community also increased after they came to the city. For instance, most of the participants reported that not only they started using these web platforms designed explicitly for the LGBTQ community but also the time spent on mobile dating applications and websites that enabled them to meet other queer individuals in the physical world increased exponentially after they came to the metropolitan city. Further, some individuals also refrained from using these dating applications and websites while in their hometown or village because there were not many people active on these applications and websites in these regions. Also, there was a fear that their identity may be revealed if they meet someone from their locality, as people in small town and villages were perceived to have a wider reach in terms of knowing others in their locality.
2. Classification on the bases of co-habitants: It was interesting for us to see the journey of queer individuals with the integration of technology in their lives and the identities that they had on the internet and social media platform. In fact, we also noted that after coming to the city, individuals who had limited access to these platforms were much more active on these platforms as compared to individuals

who had majorly stayed most of their life in these metropolitan cities. Another important factor that affected this integration and presence on the internet and social media that enabled them to live/perform their queer identities was dependent on the co-habitants that these individuals stayed with. Most individuals who were in their early career and had moved to the city were staying independently or with other young individuals who had moved to the city just like them for work. Few had also reported that though initially they were staying or were in touch with some of their relatives staying in the city, they eventually moved out as they wanted to be more independent and live a life which was close to their identity. Being independent and not being surrounded by family members/relatives was one of the reasons that these individuals were able to explore more of the queer side of the city. Though these cities offered unofficial meeting points to gay men, it was more convenient for these individuals to meet other queer individuals like them through the internet, social media platforms and dating applications. Further, individuals identifying with lesbian, bisexual and transgender identities also reported to preferred first interacting with potential partners online or through informal meeting groups organised in the city by the queer community. Overall, individuals who identified as lesbian and/or transgender felt safe meeting other individuals for romantic relationships or getting access to any information related to sexuality through online mediums as compared to the physical meetings organised by the queer community due to the domination of gay men in these spaces. The most interesting aspect for us was to see how individuals who had stayed most of their lives in rural India and were not using the internet and social media platforms started integrating these technologies in their daily lives while spending their time in the city. Individuals who were out to their families were able to use these applications and platforms without much fear; at the same time, individuals who were staying with their families in the cities and were not out used these platforms with much more caution. Overall, the independence that the city had to offer along with technological infrastructure gave many individuals an opportunity to get a taste of their real identities and lives that they had desired from a very long time at least in some of the spaces.

All the participants that we interviewed for the research had access to mobile technology, internet and social media platforms. We wanted to explore the rise of a new level of personal and professional transparency due to the integration of and access to these technologies and platforms. According to the blog, "History of Terminations and Firing Because of Employee Social Media," written by Jessica Miller-Merrell (2013), more than 60 employees were fired from their work from the year 2007 to 2014 due to some online activity that was considered offensive by their employers. A prospective applicant should not be surprised if the organisation that they have applied for a job scans their social networking websites such as Facebook and Twitter to know more about the applicant. Though our participants did not think that their organisation had used social media platforms to screen them before providing them with the opportunity, they did mention that they had many colleagues and superiors from their workplace who were in the virtual network of these participants.

Further, they also felt that it would not be challenging for them to find out about their social media activity as most of them had not filtered access to the content creation, consumption and overall activates on the internet. During the interview, when we asked one of the participants if their colleagues and other employees at their workplace had access to her social media platform, she replied:

> *Yes, many of my colleagues follow me on Facebook and Twitter. I am also very vocal about LGBTQ issues on these platforms. But it never occurred to me that they will also judge me for what I do on these social network platforms. I have filtered my family members but it never occurred to me that my colleagues could also be a problem. Now that I am thinking about it, I will filter some of my colleagues.*

Our intention for asking this question was not to warn or caution the participant, but this question gave this participant an opportunity to reflect about their online footprints and its visibility to other people at their workplace or any other person who has access to the internet. In the latter part of the chapter, we will also discuss the way many individuals have suffered from adverse consequences for having/performing a queer identity online but before that, we will see how these technologies, the internet, social media and online dating platforms have helped the LGBTQ community in India.

Internet Gave Me an Identity

Most of our participants came to know about the terminology such as—Gay, Lesbian, Bisexual, Transgender, Intersex, Queer and Asexual from the internet. Even though they were aware of their feeling, they did not know what term would be used to express their feelings or identity. It was not that they had never heard these words before, but they felt that they could understand these words in the true sense after being exposed to the internet. It was only through the internet that they could learn the global queer language and know what would be their preferred sexual orientation or gender identity label. The internet not only made these participants aware about the terms that are used to describe these identities but also opened them to new information related to these identities and lives and conditions of various queer individuals around the world. It was due to exposure of the internet that these words no longer remained words, but became identities that the individuals started identifying with. The participants have some idea about what these identities would be termed in their own regional language, but they felt that expression of these identities in the commonly spoken regional language was mostly derogatory and offensive. This does not mean that all words used to express these identities in the regional language are words that put the community down and portray them in a negative light, as there are also words that may be more neutral or when used are not loaded extensively with socio-cultural judgements towards the community. The participant did not know any of these neutral or friendly words in their own language even when they belonged to the community, as these words were not commonly used and discussed as even today talking about sexuality, sexual orientation and gender identity is tabooed in most of the structures.

Further, since these discussions are not considered "normal," over a period of time, many words were not used in the common discourse. The fact that most people and at times, even insiders from the community, do not know the words to describe their identities also tells us a lot about the importance and relevance that these issues have in a society. Since the larger Indian society has looked down upon sexual minorities and non-normative identities, these words have been used in a derogatory manner to describe a section of the society. Also, the Indian queer community have not been able to reclaim and use these regional words to describe these identities like some of the feminist and the queer movements in the western countries. The ones that have attempted to reclaim these words in India are mostly academicians or activists. On the contrary, since a larger part of the Indian population is not aware about regional words that describe the non-normative gender and sexual orientation identities, it has also been one of the reasons that some people think that identifying as Gay, Lesbian, Bisexual, Transgender, Asexual, Intersex is due to western influence and is a "western way of life." It is very common that these are the same people who argue that identifying as LGBTQ is not a part of the Indian culture. This problem is not only with lack of words or lack of awareness and sensitivity towards using words for expressing non-normative gender and sexual orientation identities, but the real problem is with the entire language system being gendered in heteronormative binary.

I knew from the age of 14 that I like men, but I did not know if a man could love another man, if something like this exists or there is a problem with me. It was when I was exposed to the internet that could understand who I was. A gay man

Words such as "gay" and "queer" were also (and are still used as) a derogatory term, but due to the feminist and queer movement in the western countries, especially the US, these words were not only retained by the community but also used with pride. Since more and more from the community started using these words with pride, these words lost its derogatory status and were used more commonly in a less demining way in the larger discourse. It is not that these words have completely lost all the derogatoriness attached with them, as it also depends on how these words are used (the intent) and by whom (insider and outsider to the community), but more and more people in the western world started feeling comfortable using these words to address them as their identity. Since these words are reclaimed to an extent in the western world, people in India (mostly in metropolitan cities) belonging to the LGBTQ community also felt comfortable using the words and language to express their identity/reality to the self and others in their immediate society as compared to other regional Indian words. The exposure to these words could be possible primarily due to the internet and the globalisation of discourses. As already discussed most individuals were either not aware of the words to describe queer identity in their regional language as they did not form part of the common discourse or the words that they were aware of also included a cultural performance of non-normative gender identity that they did not identify with. For instance, the word *Hijra* or the individuals belonging to the *Hijra* community may be identified under the umbrella term transgender while describing/communicating in English language, but it is culturally very different from how a *Hijra* lives their life, their primary source of livelihood, the process of transforming (attaining *nirvana*) and the structure of family called "*gharana*" that they belong to as compared to other identities which come under the umbrella of the transgender identity. Thus, it is not surprising that though most of the individuals interviewed for this research knew about their non-normative gender and sexual orientation identity, but the words that they felt comfortable to address these identities to the self and to others was majorly due to exposure of internet and the queer movement in India.

The role of the internet did not just remain that of leading the LGBTQ individuals to terminologies and gender theories, but much more than that. It is due to the internet that many individuals also understood their rights and the laws as an Indian citizen. Further individuals got exposure to a lifestyle or a world while reading/interacting and viewing lives of other LGBTQ individuals in other countries where the law was either in favour or even worse than the law of the land in India. Since there is a lack of out and proud LGBTQ individuals in the Indian society, many participants also said that they could find queer role models or another queer individuals from the community who could guide them through the internet. To have someone who has been there or has more experience of queer non-normative life to talk to and share mostly fear and inhibitions about life, coming out, love and intimate relationships could become possible only after the advent of the internet for many. Though this was also happening in physical queer spaces but many individuals were afraid to access and, at times, even trust these spaces. Many small queer events and spaces are mushrooming in Indian metropolitan cities and there are more meeting options today for queer individuals, which was not always like this. Further, the internet and access to technology has led to the mobilisation of the LGBTQ community to a greater extent as compared to the possibilities a decade ago. This mobilisation is bringing in a diversity of representation within the LGBTQ community as earlier it was primarily dominated by gay men. Even when individuals do not or are not able to access these queer safe spaces physically, just knowing that there is a safe space and that there are many individuals who have an identity similar to theirs is a big relief to many individuals, especially those who have not disclosed their non-normative gender and sexual orientation identities in most of the spaces.

There is no denying that individuals who have access to the internet have more exposure to the LGBTQ lives and movements all around the world, but for the transgender participants it was much more than just exposure—the internet is/was a lifesaving/changing technology for them. A participant who identifies as a transsexual man and has undergone surgery felt that the internet has played a major role in educating him about sexual reassignment surgery (SRS) and the consumption of hormones. Most of the transsexual people in India start consumption of hormones without seeking advice from the doctor and it may be fatal. Since medical facilities and other required infrastructure that help individuals transition is almost non-existent or not accessible to the people, many transsexual individuals obtain hormones and other medicine from the black market. Further, most transsexual individuals who are not out, avoid going to the doctors in India due to the belief system that the doctors might not follow the ethics of non-disclosure of the case, the hospital staff in India are not trained to handle such cases with due diligence and/or the overall staff (including the doctor) may not be trained or sensitive enough to carry the process of transformation successfully as very few people get their transformation done in Indian hospitals due to the overall stigma attached with transformation of gender in the society. Also, there are very few doctors who are queer-friendly and trained in this area which further limits the access for most of the individuals who want to transform.

Most of the people who have the financial ability and some support from family and/or friends go abroad to get their transformation completed. For a large population of transsexual individuals who cannot afford transition in another country, internet is a source where they can get access to information with regard to where they would be able to get hormones or any other medication without the recommendation of a doctor or even before that just knowing details with regard to the transformation process, the cost associated with it along with the risk involved. Coming out for a transsexual individual is not similar to that of LGB individuals. Even before the transformation process starts, transsexual individuals have reported coming out to their family and at work. Some of them had to quit their work and take a break as their workplace was transphobic. Further, many of the individuals have also reported that it is common to not receive emotional or financial support from their family after they reveal their true identity and the gender that they identify with. In such difficult times, it is through the internet that most of these individuals have been able to connect with other individuals who have undergone, currently undergoing or are planning to undergo surgery like them. At the same time, these individuals also have an opportunity to connect with various NGO's, support groups, doctors and counsellors who are transgender-/queer-friendly.

Internet and coming out: Overall exposure to the lives, laws and norms of the society with regard to the LGBTQ community throughout the world along with the ability to connect with other individuals from the community has helped many individuals to take decisions regarding the disclosure or non-disclosure of their non-normative identity. Stories of coming out in India and the region that they belong to on the internet have helped them to test the waters.

An individual who identified with the community and was out in most of the spaces decided to come out on the internet through posting a post on social media platforms to let everyone know about their sexual orientation.

> *I was out in most of the spaces, but still I would keep getting questions on my sexuality. I was tired and wanted to get over these questions, so for once I thought that I will mention my sexual orientation on the social media so that most of the people who are connected with me will know that I am gay and I will not be liable for answering anyone anymore. Through this, I was also able to know people who supported me, those who mattered to me and those who didn't. I still get questions, but it is like removing a heavy burden from my chest.* A gay man

It was comparatively more comfortable for individuals who were out in most of the spaces to not hide their non-normative identity on these social media platforms. Though very few of these individuals felt the need to announce that they belong to the LGBTQ community on their profile status. Even though they were out, they were also cautious about who could track/follow their queer digital footprints to avoid conflicts in spaces or with people that they were still not comfortable coming out too. At times, we observed that individuals who were out in most of the spaces in the real world were more cautious about their activity on the internet as compared to individuals who were not out. While probing further, we understood that since the individuals who were out in most of the spaces in the real world did not feel a strong urge towards the internet or social media as the only way of expressing their gender and sexual orientation as they could do so in physical spaces as well.

> *Now I have one ID. Though I have the fake ID, I do not log in. I am also part of a queer-friendly online group as an admin member. I use my original ID now as I am more comfortable. But I do not segregate my friends and I have restricted a few of my friends whom I think they should not know because Facebook is the place where you go to make entire world as your friend.* A gay man

A few participants used technology to educate their family members. For instance, an individual would put on any news/debate/documentary related to the LGBTQ community when his family members were around and also make them watch these shows. This also gave the individuals an opportunity to know what his immediate family thought about homosexuality and the queer community. Though this strategy could have hinted at his own sexual orientation to his family, for him, this was the safest way to not only initiate a challenging conversation but at the same time also know the opinion of his family members. This gave the individual an idea with regard to the openness of his family towards the issue, at the same time, the strategies that he might use for coming out in the future. Thus, technology gave this individual a platform to initiate conversation with his family without directly starting the conversation himself.

So now whenever there is a talk show related to the LGBT community on the TV, I just put it on in my house so that people and my family members will understand. Since LGBT is a minority community, it just happens that people don't know about it. People should know what is the meaning and the difference between Lesbians, Gay, Bisexual and Transgender. A gay man

Most of our participants felt that the regional media portrayed the LGBTQ community in a more negative way to society as compared to the national and international media. Not that all national media and news channels are pro-LGBTQ rights, but some of them started covering stories about difficulties and oppression that the people from the community have to face in the society. Though the coverage of the LGBTQ issues is increasing in the national media, the discussion remains limited. These discussions are covered only when there is a significant case of discrimination and hate crime reported against the community, or there is a judgement that concerns the community or when a city organises pride events. Further, these discussions remain limited around morality, law and society. A gay man who was planning to come out to his family decided to show them few documentaries and light-hearted movies themed around the LGBTQ community. The advent in media technology gave him not only access to content related to the LGBTQ community across the globe but also screen the content that he would be showing to his family before coming out. Thus, media technology also helped him to educate and show the "good" side of being an individual form the LGBTQ community.

> When I was coming out to my parents, I showed them some movies, which helped them to understand how the life of a gay man is. Homosexuality is always shown in a negative way rather than a positive way. Like in Telugu channels they show everything which is not to be shown. A gay man

Though very few people we interacted with said that they came out on the internet and revealed their identity to the world consciously. Instead, for most, the internet has been more of a support system to get information with regard to the external environment and the way these factors in this external environment affect the lives of people after disclosing their identity in the physical world. Further, for most that were not out, internet and social media provided them a space where they could come out without coming out. It was ironical that most of our participants were able to live their "real" identity in the virtual world rather than in the real world. Most used pseudo identity to perform their non-normative gender and sexual orientation identity on the internet.

> I created a fake ID on Yahoo. I remember those days Yahoo was very prominent. You know those LGBT groups. I ended up chatting on those groups and I used to talk to random people knowing who they are, what they are, but it just gave a sense of satisfaction that there is someone like me as well. Then later I had a WhatsApp group where people just used to connect with me through WhatsApp. I had also created a fake Facebook ID and initially, I had an Orkut ID but I was too scared. Orkut was scarier for me because that time it was the first time I was using such a platform. I got to know many people who belonged to the community. I made a couple of friends and then one of my friends told me about Plant Romeo, which is one of the gay social networking dating sites. A gay man

Some of the participants, who were not out in their organisation but out in other spaces or where out only to selected people in their organisation, either used the privacy setting on such virtual platforms to communicate to people from the community or created a fake account so that they could conceal their identity. Further, a few participants who were not out said that they consciously never expressed any views that would signal towards their sexual orientation or gender identity on social networking sites such as Facebook or Twitter, but used other networking/dating sites such as PlanetRomeo and Grindr which are social networking sites exclusively for people belonging to the GBT community. Also on sites such as PlanetRomeo and Grindr, it was not necessary for people from the community to reveal their true identity. Though even on these networking sites specially designed for the LGBTQ community exposing one's identity is not compulsory, individuals prefer and trust connecting to other individuals that are providing at least partial truth about their identity as compared to someone who does not give any information. Individuals who are out in most of the spaces have to come out to a certain extent on these social networking sites.

Further, the issue of trust is now being questioned more on these networking platforms. This is because though these platforms facilitate individuals from the community to connect with each other, it could also be easily accessible by anyone who does not identify with the community. We have already seen at the beginning of this chapter, the way in which a TV NEWS channel disclosed the identities of individuals on these platforms without their consent. Even with all the risk associated with either coming out on these technology-enabled platforms or performing a non-normative gender and/or sexual orientation with a pseudo identity, most of the individuals from the community feel that the virtual world is much safer than disclosing and/or performing non-normative gender identity in the real world.

When we had started this research and wanted to interact with people from the community, the best possible way for us to connect to individuals from the LGBTQ community was through the internet-enabled platforms. There are very few individuals who are out in most of the spaces with their non-normative gender and/or sexual orientation identity. We could connect to these individuals by getting their information from the internet and establishing contact through these platforms. For our research, it was also crucial that we connected to people who are not out in most of the spaces. We could do this through the snowballing technique from meeting the individuals who were out and also by becoming a member of various LGBT groups and forums on these social networking sites. If not for these platforms, it would have been really difficult to connect to individuals from the community. Some platforms such as Facebook were more useful as compared to other platforms, as other platforms which were specifically designed for the community mostly for individuals to connect with an intention of sharing an intimate relationship.

We found that there were some generational differences with regard to the way technology and internet-enabled networking was perceived by a few of the older members of the LGBTQ community as compared to the younger members. Though not all the older LGBTQ individuals above the age of 40 years felt difficulties or discomfort using these platforms for connecting with other individuals from the community, some of them felt that these platforms were not for someone who was seeking a serious relationship.

> Though I am not active on the internet dating and all, I keep joking to my friends that younger people are quite luckier now. I think it is more of a hook-up platform. So the objective of such a platform is to hook-up and not have meaningful relationships. I can't do that, so I have always argued on that and I have also been more feminine (feminine men do not fit the stereotypical image that most gay men on these platforms want to date) and I believe in long term relationships. I am in a long-distance relationship with my partner. A gay man (aged 47 years)

We wanted to understand the underlying reasons with regard to why some of the older individuals expressed discomfort to meet other individuals or/and having a "more meaningful" relationship through the medium of internet-enabled platforms. We could understand that the following are some of the reasons for the same:

1. Overall, these individuals were late technology adopters and the use of internet-enabled technology in everyday life for connecting to other individuals from the community was limited. Further, all the older individuals whom we interviewed for our research were from an affluent class, either reported to be too overloaded with work or were uncomfortable to interact with a technology interface even for general everyday use such as paying bills or booking tickets and so on and were mostly dependent on another individual, either from their family or office to do perform these tasks.
2. Most of them were in a committed relationship with other individuals from the community (few were even married in a heterosexual relationship) and thought that these social networking sites and mobile applications were only for meeting people for casual sex.
3. It is also true to an extent that most of the individuals using these platforms, and even the way most of these platforms are designed, are primarily for sexual encounters even when most of these platforms call themselves "dating applications or website." Though it is not impossible for individuals to find someone for long-term relationships through this site, it is would not be the primary function of these applications. Further, in a country where homosexual activity is illegal, these can be the only few places where individuals from the LGBTQ community can find other individuals for basic instinct or desire of sex/love in a society which is known for suppressing these desires. Also, more and more platforms are emerging which are not

only more inclusive for the LBTQ individuals, but where people are meeting to find potential partners for the long term (even though such partnership is not legally recognised). Few younger individuals have also questioned the desire of non-normative couples/partners/ individuals to be in relationships that are very normative in nature.
4. For a few of these older individuals, who are not in a relationship, the experience of using these applications and platforms has not been good. This problem is not with these application's user interface or platforms itself but with undesirable experience with other individuals on these platforms. These older individuals have often reported that they are not considered desirable or most of the people using this application are not interested in initiating or taking a conversation further with them mostly because of the age and non-conformance with the stereotypical image of a desirable "queer" individual, especially amongst gay men within the community.

DISCRIMINATION

Development in internet and media technology has helped the LGBTQ community, but there have been various instances where people from the community had to pay the price for being themselves and performing a queer identity in the virtual world. Irrespective of the extent of integration of these technologies in the lives of the LGBTQ community, it is clear that the dependence of people on technology is only going to increase. Further, due to technological advancements and development in infrastructure more people in the coming year will have access and be dependent on these technologies. The percentage of people having access to internet technology is increasing at an exponential rate in the rural parts of India. This will also lead to the creation of new problems and one of the issues that would have to be addressed on a national level would be about educating individuals the "right" way to use and integrate these technologies in their lives. It is a common assumption that people who have access to this technology also know the "right" way of using it and are aware that they are also responsible for their activities and the use of these platforms. Though there is a difference between the real self and the virtual self, the real self is accountable for its virtual activities. In the recent past, we have witnessed many individuals facing the repercussion for expressing their views on the virtual platform. At one point of time, it seemed like expressing any political view on the social media would lead to an arrest till the

Supreme Court had to finally strike down Section 66A of the Information Technology Act which provisioned for fine and imprisonment which may extend for three years as punishment for any information/views that might be considered offensive. Though now people have more freedom for expressing their opinions on these platforms, it is ubiquitous also to see the negative impact of revocation of this judgement. Many people today are freely writing comments which are offensive. The most commonly visible example for this would be to view the extremely sexist comments on the pictures posted by any Indian actress on Instagram and/or Facebook.

Further, many of these individuals are using their real identity while posting these offensive comments. A large section of the Indian society perceives that their activities on the virtual world do not have any impact on the real world. People are not aware that even when the virtual is not considered to be real, it is at least a part of the real where individuals are/maybe held responsible for their actions on these platforms. As more numbers of people are integrating these technologies in their lives, it becomes crucial that they are also educated in the ethical considerations that one needs to maintain. Further, we would require new laws to address these issues. The US presidential election of 2016 and the use/abuse of social media by foreign actors have taught us all that new laws and governing polices would be required as our society develops continuously in terms of technology.

Individuals from the LGBTQ community have also suffered due to underestimation of the impact that the virtual world can have on their lives. Some have also accidentally revealed or hinted towards their non-normative gender identity on these platforms when they didn't intend to, after which they had to face discrimination in the "real" spaces. We interviewed four queer participants who were in the human resource role in their organisation and asked them if their organisation did a background check enabled through social media for individuals who were applying to their organisations for employment opportunities. Three participants said that their organisation did not use any social media platforms for conducting a background check and one participant said that their organisation gave the option of sending links of the LinkedIn profile and, at times, even their Instagram/Facebook profile depending on the job. For instance, if the opening was for a position related to the operations of Social Media of the organisation, then the organisation would ask the individual to send links of their online account/profile that was managed by them. The applicants for such positions were mostly judged on the performance and strategies for promotion and estimation of these online pages rather than the content unless the contents were in the extreme and were the views of the applicants themselves. Also, this organisation used LinkedIn as a platform for searching for the right candidates for some job profiles which required a particular skill set/experience requirement. Though LinkedIn highlights the educational and professional achievement of the individuals, it would not be challenging for an individual/organisation to find out the presence, views, opinion and affiliations of people on other internet-enabled platforms using the information provided on LinkedIn. In case even if organisations used these platforms for the screening of the applicants, they would not openly say it. A transgender individual who did not disclose her non-normative gender identity to the employers during the selection process had received an oral confirmation about the employment but did not receive a written offer letter after a background check was conducted by a third party agency hired by the organisation. The only communication that she received eventually was that her profile was not suitable for the role applied. Many organisations hire a third party agency for conducting a background check for the employees who have provisionally been selected for the job. These background verifications are more rigorous for the higher level posts in the organisation. There is no law governing the background verification of the employees other than the organisation is expected to have an ISO 27001 certification. Thus, it should not be surprising if an organisation or a third party organisation contracted by the organisation is scanning a prospective employee's social media.

Most of the LGBTQ individuals, especially who had not disclosed their identity, faced discrimination as a result of information revealed on the social media platform after they were employed in the organisation. It is common to connect and network with colleagues and individuals from the workplace. Further, these connections are not just limited to more professional platforms such as the LinkedIn but also to more informal ones such as Facebook, Twitter and Instagram. For instance, if a gay man would have other friends from the LGBTQ community on these social media platforms even when other people from the community who are added in this person's friends list, writes or posts something, or tag him, or the person himself likes, comments on such post then it may signal to other people in his network about the sexual orientation or gender identity of the person. Though this can be managed by modifying the privacy setting or having a different "queer profile," it may become difficult at times for a person to plan the visibility of every online activity.

A gay man we interviewed (let's call him Peter) was active on a dating platform for gay, and bisexual men was discovered by another queer employee in his organisation who also using this platform. Peter is informally out in his organisation to a few of his colleagues and was also using his real identity on this dating platform to meet other men. At the same time, the employee who discovered Peter on this dating platform was using a pseudo identity and was not out in the organisation. Peter was repeatedly asked by the closeted gay man to give him sexual favours in the organisation's washroom or he would circulate the screenshots of Peter's pictures which were uploaded on the dating site eventually with the intention of taking advantage. The organisation where Peter was working is a world's leading IT company and is known for its diversity and inclusion initiatives. Ultimately, Peter had to warn the man seeking sexual favours with formal action of filing a complaint to the human resource team. Even though the harassment stopped, Peter's identity at his workplace was compromised and this was done by another person who identified with the queer community. Peter felt that he could handle this situation as he was already informally out to few of his colleagues and that his organisation had strong diversity and inclusion policy, but he was still afraid if his "semi-nude" pictures would be circulated in the workplace.

As most of these dating platforms show the profile of other individuals with respect to geographical proximity, many queer individuals working in a large organisation have reported finding other employees who are not out but present on these platforms. Most of the times, these individuals also become friends/acquaintances with other queer colleagues on these platforms, but then one who reveals their identity on these platforms should also be prepared if their identity is revealed to people in close proximity at the workplace or any other space. The integration of technology in our lives directly or indirectly is to such an extent that it has become difficult for us to avoid its impact in our lives. Further, the reach of these technologies is to such an extent in most of the spaces that today individuals accessing the queer-friendly spaces may even unknowingly come out or signal towards their non-normative gender and sexual orientation identity. A regional newspaper printed a photograph of people attending a talk on queer identities. One of the women attending this event had to face questions and justify her presence in this event to her family as it was themed around LGBTQ identities. In another incident, two gay participants who were not out in their workplace had participated in Hyderabad pride march/protest held in the year 2014 and were covered by the regional newspaper and NEWS channels. The participation of people from the LGBTQ community and the allies in the year 2014 had decreased across India due to the regressive judgement passed by the Supreme Court in December 2013 which reinstated Section 377 of the IPC. Due to limited participation of people supporting equal rights for the LGBTQ community this year, especially in the smaller cities and due to high media coverage of the pride, some people participating in the pride got covered by the local and national news channel. The next day, the photos of these two men protesting against Section 377 along with various other people who had participated in the march were circulated in the newspapers and television channels. None of these individuals was out in their organisation and had to face questions from their colleagues. One of the individuals avoided the situation by saying that he was participating in pride as an ally as his friend was gay and he wanted to support his friend. Since the individual was cis-gender and was working in an IT organisation which was an equal opportunity provider at least on paper, he could avoid any repercussion of appearing in the media for supporting LGBTQ rights.

> *We had Hyderabad pride, and I participated in it. I didn't know that my picture has come in some newspaper; I still don't know which newspaper my picture had come because I don't read the regional newspaper. One of my friends came, and he asked me that if I had participated in the pride. I was so surprised—how did he come to know. Then I told him that 'I went as an ally with my gay friend but by that time he had spread all rumours on the company, to all my colleagues. Then my friends asked me why did I attend the pride and also advised that I should not go there as it will spoil your image and all.*

On the other hand, the other individual who was also covered by the media participating in the LGBTQ pride witnessed an increase in discrimination at his workplace to the extent that he became the victim of physical discrimination. Though not out in the organisation, he was already discriminated in his workplace by some of the colleagues due to his effeminate behaviour which did not match up with the gender identity and role of a man. The individual reported getting used to facing derogatory comments, and he did not want to file a formal complaint to the human resources as he feared that these instances will only aggravate the situation. Reporting these instances would have created more problems for him given the existing orthodox masculine culture of the manufacturing organisation for which he was working. Before being covered by the media, this individual was only facing verbal discrimination but, after this incident, a few of his colleagues even threated and assaulted him physically within the workplace premises.

According to Goffman (1963), the main issue with an individual facing stigma is managing information about their stigma and not that of managing tension generated during social contacts. Goffman writes,

> The issue is not that of managing tension generated during social contacts, but rather that of managing information about his failing. To display or not to display; to tell or not to tell; to let on or not to let on; to lie or not to lie; and in each case, to whom, how, when, and where.

From the above paragraph, we can infer that the onus of managing information related to the stigma is the responsibility of the individual. According to Sharma (2014), people have an opportunity to perform their identity on such virtual platforms even more strongly. Further, Sharma adds that most of the people do not consciously construct an identity on the online spaces. That means the way people perform or want to perform their identity(ies) in real life leads to the formation of a similar kind of identity(ies) on the virtual spaces as well. This might become a problem especially for people who are not out in the real world. The individual who has a fear of being stigmatised consciously creates passing strategy to avoid uncomfortable situations. It may not always be possible for an individual to be conscious all the time even on the virtual space. Even when the individual attempts to control the flow of information on virtual spaces, there is no guarantee that such information would be safe and not accessible to other parties. Further, there are always external factors which are not in control of the individual. Like in case of the individual who had attended the pride protest and was covered in the local newspaper and media which ultimately became the reason for aggravation of the discrimination that he was already facing. This individual thought that their identity at the pride was different from the identity performed in the workplace and thus did not expect an intersection of these identities. People have multiple identities, and some identities may become more prominent in some spaces compared to other spaces. For example, an individual who is not out with their non-normative gender and sexual orientation at their workplace may try to suppress/hide their queer identity at the workplace, but at the same time may not suppress this identity at pride or spaces which are considered to be safe for the LGBTQ community.

Goffman gave the example of a man being a father to his son and the same individual being an employee in the organisation. Here, even though the person remains the same, his identity (or one of the identities predominantly performed) in both the places is not the same. Similarly, people from the community had a different identity when with the people from the queer community as compared to that at their workplace. While being with the individuals from the LGBTQ community in spaces that are heteronormative as well as spaces that may be considered as safe space for the community, we noticed that there is a change in performance of queer identities for not only people who are not out but also people who are out in heteronormative spaces.

Due to increased interdependency on technologies, different identities of people are/may be represented at the same place/time may be problematic at times. Further, the network that the individual has in different spheres of life would also come at one single place or at least intersect each with different spaces, often leading to problems and complications that the individual may not have anticipated. Some respondent believed that their identity in front of the members of the queer community was their "real" identity, whereas the identity that they were portraying at their workplace was different. The physical world and the virtual world may not be considered the same by an individual and the individual may have different identity in such spaces, but if the creation of such an identity is not done with a conscious mind, then the identity of individuals in the virtual and the real world may overlap and be similar, if not identical. When people differentiate the virtual and the real world, they forget that the virtual world is part of the real world. In such cases, it would become very difficult for individuals with stigma to control the flow of information. Further, it would be equally difficult for an individual who has been exposed and is dependent on such technologies to withdraw themselves from such virtual spaces completely. It may have been easier for the individual to control the flow of information in the 1960s, but today the conditions are different. Individuals become parts of various public and private databases and it is not very difficult for others to extract such information. In such cases, even when the individual uses passing strategies, it may not always be possible to control and manage the flow of information. We have also seen in this research that technology has played a role in the lives of the queer people. We have to understand that the virtual and the real world are not different from each other; that the virtual world is part of the real world. Thus, any actions, either by the individual or by a third party, would impact the life of the individuals as they would not have total control over the flow of information. A lot of change, especially in the context of technology, in the world today has been witnessed from the time when these stigma management and information flow theories were given. It has become important to identify, and answers questions related to the flow of information in the "age of information technology" and accordingly introduce changes in the theories.

When the Supreme Court reinstated the Section 377 of IPC in December 2013, an organisation send an email to all its employees stating even with the new judgement, the organisation would strive hard to provide their LGBTQ employees safe space. Further, the organisation mentioned that all identities are respected and that the organisation will always be there for their employees even in tough times. When we interviewed an individual from this organisation, he felt secured and knew that at least his workplace where he spends the maximum of his productive time is queer-friendly and supports LGBTQ rights, even in a country where the external environment is not in favour of the community. Further, this individual also said that he would not leave the job and join another organisation because he felt safe and accepted in his current organisation. This organisation does not have a lot of budget for their diversity and inclusion initiative, but they regularly communicate with their employees through email and other technology-enabled platforms. Sending emails about the values that the organisation believes to all its employees did not cost much to the organisation, but the impact of using these internet technologies on the employees of this organisation was high. The organisation could communicate to its employees on a sensitive issue like the LGBTQ rights and since this communication was marked for all the employees, even individuals who were not out felt safe. This also gave heterosexual employees an opportunity to understand the stand of their organisation with respect to the inclusion and diversity of the LGBT community and the steps to becoming a better ally. There are organisations which are now making use of technology-enabled platforms to initiate difficult conversations. One of the organisations created a virtual platform which gave their employees an opportunity to express their views, thoughts or concerns on this platform. Though there was a screening mechanism for the comments on this platform, the employees had the option of not disclosing their identity while initiating a conversation on this platform. An employee from this organisation who had not revealed their identity at the workplace had started the discussion on the inclusion and diversity of LGBTQ employees in the workplace through this platform. He did not want to come out in the organisation or hint towards his non-normative identity while having this conversation, thus this platform was a perfect fit to know about the stand of the employees in the organisation without disclosing his own identity.

To conclude, even when performing the "real" identity in the virtual platform has had repercussions, many individuals from the community still feel that the virtual space is safer compared to the real space. Organisations can make innovative use of the virtual space to communicate to their employees that their organisation is a safe space and initiate diversity and inclusion for their employees.

REFERENCES

Goffman, Erving. 1963. *Stigma*. London: Penguin.

Miller-Merrell, Jessica. 2013, May 7. *History of Terminations & Firings Because of Employee Social Media*. http://www.blogging4jobs.com/social-media/history-of-terminations-firings-employee-social-media/#VLCwk51STwld3Kbt.97. Accessed 8 December 2014.

Sharma, Ditilekha. 2014. *Queer Expressions in the Online Space*. Higher Education Innovation and Research Applications (HEIRA) Programme, Centre for the Study of Culture and Society and Centre for Internet and Society, Bangalore as Part of an Initiative on 'Mapping Digital Humanities in India.'

CHAPTER 5

Are Indian Organisations Safe for the LGBTQ Employees?

We were able to interact with many Queer individuals during the research process, but it was sad to know that only a few of them were working in organisations that had inclusion and diversity policy for the LGBTQ individuals. To be precise, only six of the employees said that they had a diversity and inclusion policy designed explicitly for LGBTQ employees in their organisation. None of the other participants had ever worked in an organisation which had inclusive policies or were not aware of their organisation's stand on the issue of LGBTQ rights. Further, the organisations which had these LGBTQ policies addressed only cases of discrimination and harassment. LGBTQ couples/unions often face inequality when it comes to compensation benefits, medical benefits, life insurance, social security, income tax and welfare payments, which are accessible only to heterosexual married couples. Even organisations which have policies in India have not recognised survivor benefits in occupational pensions and compensations schemes, thus continuing differential treatment for queer employees. Further, employees working in these organisations felt that either these policies were never really translated into praxis or, at most, what their organisation did was very tokenistic as part of these diversity initiatives in the form of seminars/talks and an informal network of LGBTQ employees in the workplace. However, at least having a policy specifically designed for the LGBTQ individuals gave employees identifying with the community a sense of security that their organisation recognised and formally communicated that LGBTQ rights are also human rights. There was just one participant who was working in an organisation which provided partner benefits to homosexual/non-normative couples, but if any person from the LGBTQ community wanted to avail these employment benefits, they were formally required to disclose their identity to their employers.

At times, it is also possible that an organisation has inclusive policies, but the employees working in these organisations were not aware of these policies. While interacting with two participants who worked in the same organisation, we came to know that one was aware of a written policy for the LGBTQ employees, whereas the other individual was not aware if any such policy existed in the organisation. Even when these organisations have written policy for the LGBTQ inclusion, they are not communicated to the employees due to various reasons. The scenario in these workplaces is no different from that of any teacher in an Indian school skipping chapters on the human reproductive system. The primary reasons for not clearly having a discussion around this issue and policies are that hardly any managers are well informed about the community themselves, the perception of these people are based on bias even when the policy is drafted to address biases arising from heteronormativity, and most individuals in leadership positions do not consider this communication relevant due to the assumed heterosexuality of all their employees and for not having visibly queer people in the organisation who are out to most of the people in the organisation.

A few organisations did not have a written policy on diversity and inclusion of individuals from the community, but were able to facilitate safe spaces for their employees even without these policies. It was in these organisations that some individuals were able to come out and be proud of their identity as they felt welcomed and accepted by their colleagues in the workplace. Almost all these organisations were small or medium sized and had people in leadership positions that were pro-LGBTQ rights. These organisations did not account for survivor benefits for the partners of the LGBTQ individuals, but aimed at proving safe space to any employees who identified with queer identities. The individuals who came out in these organisations were already out in a few other spaces as well, and thus were comfortable to disclose their identity when the organisation provided a safe space for them.

> *We do not have a policy for inclusion of LGBT employees but let me clarify that we have a very supportive environment. But let me also clarify that supportive in the sense that it does not offer any support with respects to partners benefits*

that straight people get but in terms of working and work environment, it is not a thing. I am actually one of the many gay people working in the company. A gay participant

Not having a written policy most of the time adds to the confusion amongst individuals from the LGBTQ community with regard to the stand of their organisation and LGBTQ rights. In such organisations, individuals who are out in other spaces try to test the water if it would be safe for LGBTQ individuals. Individuals who are not out often try to guess if their colleagues or supervisors are supportive and try to draw cues from indirect questions about the community or even with respect to their stand on the rights of women in the society. Often, the individuals end up concluding that the organisation that they are working for does not care about LGBTQ individuals.

Before the Supreme Court had decriminalised Section 377 for consenting adults in November 2018, I was invited by a multinational organisation operating in India for consultation with regard to the scope of an LGBTQ diversity and inclusion (D & I) initiative. Even after I explained to the vice president of human resources the implications of Section 377 multiple times and that the law did not restrain organisations in India to not have such initiatives, the organisation decided that they will not take up the issue of LGBT employees as it was "too risky" for them! I started questioning if it was really risky for this organisation like many other organisations to take a D & I initiative for the LGBTQ community or they wanted to save themselves from "work" which was considered neither necessary nor legally mandatory in the first place. Even after the Supreme Court decriminalised consensual same-sex activity, all that this organisation did was an "internal" event where they wanted to screen a short movie which had to be less than 15 minutes. They kept this event extremely "internal," that too just for few selected employees. From my experience, this looked more like a facade where the organisation just wanted to conduct any event related to LGBTQ diversity, without even involving all of their employees nor with an intention of sensitising them or making the organisations safe, but to show it to the head office located in the US that they are indeed equal opportunity employers.

During the research, we observed in the name of diversity and inclusion most organisations are doing nothing more than complying with the labour laws (at times, even finding it difficult to comply with necessary industrial relations and labour laws), and projecting it as their D & I initiative. It was not surprising that for most organisations Section 377 of the IPC became an excuse for not having D & I initiatives for LGBTQ individuals.

Organisations treat people from the LGBTQ community as abnormal and inferior due to the hostile attitude of the state towards the community (Concannon 2008). As same-sex families are not accounted for by the state, even the organisations do not account for equal rights to LGBTQ employees in the work-family policies (Beauregard et al. 2007). This makes sexual orientation diversity one of the least important factors for organisations outside the US (Goodman 2013). Organisations operating in India can play an essential role in providing safe spaces to the LGBT community. Since sexual orientation is not visible and is implied on the performativity of gender role and identity, one cannot assume an individual's sexual orientation and gender identity based on common stereotypes. Thus, organisations cannot and should not justify their decision to have an inclusion and diversity initiative for the individuals from the community based on just the number of people who are out or on the visibility for the queer individuals within the organisation. Further, Section 377 does not stop Indian organisations from having an inclusion and diversity initiative for the LGBTQ community. These days, we hear a lot of HR managers in leadership positions use the phrase "Diversity is being invited to the party; Inclusion is being asked to dance" coined by V. Myers (2015). When one belongs to the LGBTQ community in a country like India, diversity is not a party but a fight to have fundamental human rights and inclusion is survival. Let us understand Section 377 which has been cited as one of the prominent reasons by most of the organisations for not taking D & I initiative for the LGBTQ community till September 2018:

Section 377 from the year 2013 to 2018 read as follows:

377. Unnatural Offences: Whoever voluntarily has carnal intercourse against the order of nature with any man, woman or animal shall be punished with imprisonment for life, or with imprisonment of either description for a term which may extend to ten years, and shall also be liable to fine.

According to this section of the IPC, any sexual act other than penile-vaginal sex even between two consenting adults was a criminal offence as it was considered as intercourse against the order of nature. This meant that the section was applicable to any individual irrespective of their sexual orientation. So even when an adult heterosexual couple is indulging in any sexual activity other than penile-vaginal sex, it was considered against the order of nature. To put it simply, a heterosexual couple indulging in "oral" or "anal" sex may also be considered as offenders under this section as it was intercourse against the order of nature. So why is it that Section 377 is looked as a law applicable only to the LGBTQ community and not the heterosexuals population in India? This is primarily due to two main reasons:

1. Most of the people were not aware about the interpretation of this law and how it has an equal interpretation for heterosexual individuals, but most cis-gender heterosexual individuals are ignorant about it as a result of privilege that one has in society for performing their gender in a normative manner. As a result of this privilege of being cis-gender heterosexual, most individuals are ignorant about the law (even when they are partially aware about it), as any sexual activity that a cis-gender heterosexual couple performs is normalised in the society. An example of this would be normalisation of marital rape in Indian society.
2. The issue of Section 377 has been taken up by the LGBTQ community in their protest and their narratives, as it is one of the factors that have contributed to their exploitation, discrimination and vulnerability. Since the LGBTQ community is vocal about this section and has raised this issue time and again, it appears to the normative population of the society that this issue is an issue faced only by the LGBTQ community.

Even when Section 377 was reinstated by the Supreme Court in 2013, it did not criminalise a person identifying themselves as homosexuals or identifying with the queer community, but only criminalises the sexual activities other than penile-vaginal intercourse as a criminal offence. The important thing to remember for all of us is that this law was applicable to all the people including heterosexuals who indulge in sexual activity other than penile-vaginal sex. Further, gender being fluid, it could also be argued that a heterosexual individual may also involve themselves in same-sex activity. Since this law was old, vague and open to interpretations, many researchers have suggested that it will not be applicable to a woman in sexual activity with another woman as they cannot have intercourse due to their inability to penetrate. It is only when men are caught in the act of sex they could be prosecuted with this law. For a very long time it was an irony that in the largest democratic country the punishment for raping a woman is seven years, but for loving someone from the same gender was minimum ten years.

Section 377 was used as a shield by the organisations, not to have any active attempts of making the workplace inclusive and safe for the LGBTQ employees in India during this period between 2013 and 2018 till the five-judge bench finally decriminalised it. It was not that majority of organisations did not or were not capable of understanding the law, but just that they did not see any point in even making attempts to understand/interpret the law and the situation of the LGBTQ employees.

For the organisation, it means the following:

1. It was/is not illegal to conduct diversity and inclusion initiative for the LGBTQ community at the workplace.
2. Organisations can have formal and/or informal LGBTQ support groups/networks within their organisation.
3. Since sexual orientation is not visible, organisations do not have to wait for LGBT employees to come out to start D & I initiatives.
4. Organisations should know that it is not necessary that just because they are conducting D & I initiatives, people from the community will come out. Coming out is a big decision and everyone has their own journey of coming out. Organisations should respect this decision and not assume or out an employee's non-normative gender identity or sexual orientation based on common stereotypes.
5. People in leadership positions and human resource managers should learn more about the community and understand different identities within the community along with intersectionality of these identities and create a gender-neutral/gender-friendly language with gender-neutral/gender-safe spaces that can be created before starting the D & I initiative.

Even today that Section 377 is no more applicable to consensual same-sex adults, most organisations do not want to invest time and energy to bring in inclusive policies and equality for the LGBTQ community, as the majority of times these issues are seen as trivial and unnecessary to be discussed in the workplace. Managers see it as an extra burden and a work which does not result or impact directly in overall productivity. For a very long time, lack of sensitivity could not be officially stated as a reason by the organisation for avoiding inclusion initiatives for the community, the easiest way out was by labelling anything to do with individuals/communities identifying with the LGBTQ community as illegal. But this is not just the case with LGBTQ diversity. This is the approach for most of the

Indian organisations with overall importance of any diversity and inclusion initiative. Other than diversity and inclusion activities for women, most of the organisations do not have any policies or initiatives for any other vulnerable or minority individuals/groups in society. Most of the D & I policies for other minority groups in the society remain just on paper, worst not even on paper many times. So why are organisations in India doing D & I activities for women? Are they really concerned about the inequality that women have to face in the society or at the workplace? Most organisations conduct diversity and inclusion initiatives for women in India not because they really believe in empowerment and equality of women, but because there are laws that mandate organisations to follow certain guidelines to protect the interest of women in the society. It was also thought that organisations had slowed down the hiring of women after the "me too" movement in India. It was interesting that organisations found it easier to remove women from the workplace rather than addressing the root cause or even the sexual harassment offenders. Majority of the times, these organisations' diversity and inclusion revolves around these laws of lands and critical analysis of the initiatives tells us that most organisations are just following the law in the name of D & I activates.

ARE SOME INDUSTRIES MORE ACCEPTING THAN OTHERS?

We often come across statements such as "all (male) fashion designers are gay!" In this segment, we would explore if there is any truth to such statements or they are mere stereotypes. Also, it is believed that maximum gay people work either in fashion or in media. Is the fashion and media industry more gay-/queer-friendly as compared to other industries? Or are there other industries as well which are as accepting as these industries? Is fashion, film and media accepting of the queer people and if not then why is it that most of the times visible gay/queer people are perceived to be from such industries. To find answers to these questions, we asked the respondents questions related to their industry and the organisation where they were working. In the first section of the questions we attempted to know what was the perception of the participants about such stereotypical statements and if they really thought that some industries were more accepting than others and, in the second section, our focus was to explore the importance of working in spaces/industries that are perceived to be safer as compared to other spaces/industries.

The participants we interviewed were working in fashion, media, public relations, event management organisations, educational institutes, IT and ITES, medicine and pharmaceutical, banking and insurance, retail, consulting, automobile, aviation and manufacturing organisations. Though most of our participants were from the private sector, we also tried to include participants from the public sector. Further, all of these individuals had worked or were working in formal/organised sectors.

Even though it is commonly stereotyped that there are more LGBTQ individuals in fashion and media, most of our participants even those who were working in these industries thought that this statement was based on common stereotypes mostly because more queer individuals were visible in these industries. The participants working in fashion or media thought that these industries might be perceived to be LGBTQ-friendly, but in reality, individuals have to face discrimination, especially those involved in operational level work. While the discrimination in the operational level is very blatant, the discrimination in middle and strategic levels of these organisations was more indirect and subtle. Our participants thought that the reasons some industries such as media and fashion are perceived to be more LGBTQ-friendly as compared to other industries are as follows:

1. The nature of some professions is such that it becomes easier for the person to come out. For instance, a gay fashion designer who specialises in women's clothing and dressing would not have any problems working with the opposite gender. The Indian fashion industry is dominated by men, as from designers to tailors most of the individuals are men. When there are limited options, women clients are relatively comfortable with gay/queer fashion designers as there is no or limited perceived sexual tension with men in fashion who have a non-normative identity. Even when gay men are portrayed in the fashion industry, then they are shown to have effeminate attributes dressed colourfully like a woman. Another example for the same can be that a gay doctor would find it difficult to come out because there might be a possibility that men might not be comfortable with a gay doctor "touching" them. This can be inferred with the fact that still in India, the majority of the women prefer a female doctor over a male doctor as they feel comfortable with a female doctor. Similarly, men might not feel comfortable around a gay doctor and women anyway have a preference to consult woman doctor over a male doctor irrespective

of their sexual orientation. As a gay man or queer person who is out in the open, his identity, ability and knowledge are continuously challenged by society. When we say the word doctor or surgeon, the picture of a "man" comes in our mind. Similarly, when we think about the job of a nurse we imagine a woman. When a man comes out as "gay," he is degraded from the top position of the hierarchy that men occupy in our patriarchal society and since gay men are considered to have feminine attributes, their status comes down to that of a woman and most of the times even below that. We have already seen in the previous chapters of discrimination that people from the community who are "visible" as queer or are out, have a higher probability of being exposed to harassment and discrimination.

2. Another reason which was cited by some of the participants was that gay men are more inclined towards the creative side as they do not think in the binary. Such statements from the participants made us introspect if gay men were perceived to be more creative than straight men. Thus, we also asked our participants questions like if they felt that gay men were more creative or had better negotiation skills or any other skills over and above the straight men to know about the insider perceptions for the same. Again, it is stereotyped in our society that as gay a man is effeminate, they would also be as "emotional" as a woman and have the skills that a woman would have. This makes gay men "weaker" than the straight men. At the same time, lesbian women are stereotyped to be masculine or butch and thus are considered stronger than the straight women. The household model also notes the same. A gay participant who is out in the open and heads the communication department in his organisation said:

> *That is probably true. The stereotype is based on some truth. Fashion, Bollywood, jewellery designing and creative careers are more likely to have LGBT people just because LGBT turns to be more creative. If you go to ONGC, Coal India, SAIL and so on then you are less likely to see openly gay people. Probably because the acceptance level in the industry is very low. So I do not know why gay people get into creative spaces, but I know a lot of engineers who do MBA and move in marketing or HR or who do a MA and go into arts. Creativity requires you to have an open mind. Engineering and field like that where there is logic, it kind of trains you to think logically which is good but it also restricts you to think in dichotomy. Either right or it's not right. So mathematical mindset tends to look at the world with a binary but creativity requires you to be so imaginative.*

3. The third reason which came up while interviewing respondents was that gay men in media and fashion who are at the top of the hierarchy are visible because they are always in focus or "limelight," as they are working in media, fashion and filmmaking. Queer people in any industry who are not at the top of the hierarchy hardly get attention from media. This is also true for queer people at the operational level of the glamour industry. Further, people from other industries do not have as much fame and coverage as compared to people working in the glamour industry. When the CEO of Apple, Tim Cook, came out and disclosed his sexual orientation identity on the public platform the news was covered by media across the world, but if a gay person from a small organisation would have come out, it would not have been covered by the global or even local media. Tim Cook is not the only CEO who is out; there have been many others in a leadership position who have come out and revealed their sexual orientation identity. A gay participant who is a fashion designer and has his label said:

> *There are so many gay men all over...you just have to get on to a gay app and you will know (laughs). I think people focus more on individuals who are doing well especially in fashion, entertainment or media.*

A gay participant who worked in an advertisement organisation firm had suffered derogatory remarks and was often discriminated. It is not necessary that people who work in media are entirely accepted. Here, we should understand that visibility in industry and acceptance in the same industry may not be related with each other. It is also possible that the chances of discrimination in media and fashion industry, especially for men who have feminine attributes irrespective of their sexual orientation, would be more as compared to other industries because of the stigma attached with such a work profile. The respondent said:

> *I am in the Bollywood so there are a lot of people in the media, they are actually open about their sexuality. And people in this industry know that there are people who belong to the LGBT community. And that such kind of people exists. See there are two things, the first is to accept that these people are there and the second thing is that do you respect them or not?*

Though some roles/job profiles may give an individual an opportunity to come out or be visibly queer, it does not mean that there will be any less discrimination of these individuals. Further, due to the spillover effect it might also happen that this individual might be discriminated in other spaces of life as compared to an individual who is closeted or not out in their workplace. Though we know that there is a higher possibility of adverse economic and social implications on an individual who comes out and discloses their non-normative gender and sexual orientation identity at the workplace, we do not know if there are positive economic and social implications of being queer in some roles, such as fashion designer or in some industries such as media. Further, the discrimination for individuals who are out or visible in these industries/roles is different from that of people who are not out in their organisation and/or not visibly queer.

A transsexual woman who was undergoing transformation and working in a film production company felt that she was discriminated at the set. Most of the people handling the operational duties on the set were not aware and sensitised on these issues. Thus, as the transsexual woman was visibly queer, she had to suffer a lot of discrimination, stares and derogatory remarks were part of her routine work. The participant said:

> On the contrary, media is more backward. Directors, producers, executive producers are the only people on the set who are educated and the rest of the people like the set boy, light man, and cameraman are mostly not aware. They will not respect you. They will call you names. So in media also there is discrimination. However, the fashion industry is different. Logo ye he sochte hai ke fashion me to sirf gay log kaam karte hai. (People think that only gay men work in the fashion industry.)

Time and again, we have seen gay men being represented in the form of humour and in the form of mental sickness in the mainstream Hindi cinema. There are very few mainstream Hindi movies that have broken these stereotypical representations of gay men and shown the complexities that gay people have to deal with. The "hero" of the movie is depicted as someone who is very masculine and has the strength to tackle numerous people in a fight scene. Male masculinity is magnified in these movies and, rarely, there are instances that people have talked about female masculinity in their movies and even if the topic of female masculinity is touched upon in some movies then it is depicted that a women can be "an object of desire" only when she "acts as an ideal women." Even though limited and not respectful, gay characters have had some screen time in mainstream cinema as compared to the LBTQ community. Further, there are various instances of casting couch and sexual harassment in the film industry. Not only women but also men have been subjected to such harassment. In such cases, we can only question how each individual defines the term "acceptance." For an individual, acceptance by an industry may be equated to visibility, for some it is getting a livelihood and others it is being treated equally at par with the heterosexual people. A participant said:

> *There is never an institute which is open and out, there are people in the institute who are open and out.*

The second question which was asked to the participants was that if they were harassed in their organisation would they be willing to change their organisation/industry to an organisation/industry which was considered gay-friendly, but giving them a lower pay/position/different profile than what they were receiving from their previous company in which they had to face discrimination due to their sexual orientation. Interestingly, all the gay participants who were out in their organisation by choice said that they would not leave the company without receiving a proper explanation and question the bases of sexual orientation becoming the reason for discrimination. Not only this, but the participants who were out in their organisation also confronted people who passed sexist remarks or used a derogatory term to identify or define the people from the community. A participant who is out in his organisation said:

> *If somebody harassed me then I will make sure that I fully harass them. I will not leave him. Because I am at a point in my life that I am not scared or anything...so I would make sure that the person definitely gets his reward back that I would make it very clear because I don't think that anybody has the right and being in HR...I know the policies. I do not think I will allow anyone even to harass. He will get his due back for sure. And I am not going to leave my organisation because somebody is harassing me as leaving would be like giving up. I will leave the organisation if I want to not because somebody harasses me.*

It is to be noted that the organisation where this individual was working had separate inclusive and diversity policy for the LGBTIQ community and also the organisation had zero tolerance for any discrimination based on gender or sexual orientation. So this participant was already working in one of the few organisations which had an anti-discrimination policy to protect the rights of the LGBTQ community.

Participants who were closeted felt that if they were discriminated on the basis of their gender, then they would change the organisation/industry. Most of these closeted individuals felt that they would work even for a lower pay given the fact that they were assured that gender and sexual orientation-based discrimination would not take place. This means that participants who were not out in their workplace either had decided consciously that they would want to conceal their identity at the workplace or were not sure about the environment of the organisation and perceived the fact that their organisation would not accept their sexual orientation. For individuals from the community who were out only to a few people in their organisation, factors such as the perception and actual level and extend of discrimination, cost of opportunity for leaving the current work, financial stability and career growth became the deciding factors that would help them make the decision if they would switch to another organisation/industry which was more inclusive for the LGBTQ community. These participants felt that they would leave the organisation/industry only in extreme and intolerable cases of discrimination. The same was not true in the case of individuals who identified as transgenders. Transsexuals who had undergone surgery or who are undergoing transformation were willing to change not only the organisation/industry but also the job profile if the organisation was queer-friendly. All the transsexual respondents expressed that it was tough in the first place to get an employment opportunity and once they got employed, discrimination in some or the other form was certain. Most of the respondents felt that India has still not reached a stage where the LGBTIQ community could be easily accepted in society. But there have been cases where even transgender employees are now accepted in their organisation for who they are. During the research, I became a member of various LGBTIQ forums on Facebook. In one of those fora, I saw a post by a transsexual man named Sameer (name changed). In that post, Sameer had shared a letter which his company CEO had given him, which said:

> It may take some time for us to get used to the idea of calling you Sameer, and we may also refer to you in the feminine gender. Please do not take offence. With time, we will all get used to the new name.

CAN LGBTQ EMPLOYEES LEAD ORGANISATIONS?

People tell you that what will he lead us when he cannot lead his own life.
—A transsexual participant

Most of the participants felt that they would not be respected in leadership roles in top management in Indian organisations if they were out with their non-normative identities. It was surprising that even the individuals who were out by choice in their workplace felt that even though they had disclosed their identity, their sexuality and gender would cause a hindrance with regard to how people view them as leaders. Most individuals from the community who were already in leadership roles and were out felt that even when the role required them to lead and direct their subordinates, they were not as respected or able to develop a close relationship with their subordinates. It was partly because they thought that they were not respected and could not be role models for heteronormative individuals and also because these individuals did not want to disclose too much of their personal life due to the fear that it will lead to further judgement and isolation as their lives were certainly nowhere close to a heteronormative monogamous lifestyle that is considered moral by a large part of the society. Some also felt that they might be respected to their face due to the power structure/relation within the organisation but not "really" respected in the true sense. These individuals often felt that they had to deal with issues which other leaders did not face because of their sexual orientation or visible queer characteristics. Even when the participants displayed effective leadership qualities, their non-normative sexual orientation and gender identity was used against them by their colleagues who considered them competition or a potential threat.

> *Even when I am promoted as a leader, I think my subordinates will not accept me as I will always be considered an outsider and will not be able to maintain synergy with all of them.* A gay participant

Individuals who were in leadership roles and were not out in their organisation felt that there was too much at stake to lose for them if they came out and disclosed their identity. At the same time, it was interesting to see that individuals from their community who had just started their career felt that it was easier to come out when one is in a leadership position as there is a certain power that the individual has and is also able to have some financial stability by the time they reach these positions. Most individuals who were not out and were in the initial stage of their career thought that they might come out in the organisation once they were at a more stable position and had grown within the organisation, as the organisation that they are working with would also view them as an asset. Individuals who identified as lesbian or transgender thought that the fight for them was to have a place and be respected for their work in the workplace. Being in a leadership role and also being respected with their non-normative sexual orientation and/or gender identity was a distant dream.

In our country, most people find it difficult to respect women in a leadership position. If on top of that the women comes out as a lesbian or an individual identifies as a trans-person then all hell will break loose. A lesbian woman

There were only eight participants (all gay men) in leadership roles in their organisation who felt that they were respected as leaders despite being out and that it was their leadership ability along with the ability to deliver results that was main factor determining if they were looked up to by their subordinates and colleagues rather than their non-normative sexual orientation and gender identity. Interestingly, we observed that individuals from the community thought that they had an advantage over heterosexual married men as they could put in more time at their work and towards their career growth and development due to lesser/no commitment from family, wife and children like most heterosexual individuals.

Gay people can be good leaders as compared to other straight people as straight people have so many commitments and all that stuff about family life, children. Even we have our own family life but we don't have that much commitments and we don't have all that typical relationships...you know...we don't have to take care of our children and pay their college fees and all as so we don't have and can't have a typical relationships and that family tension and persons from your wife and mom-in-law, dad-in-law...so we can concentrate on our work and growth. Just because they are feminine they are bad leaders there is nothing like that. In fact, gay people know and are good at people's management as they can read both male and female mindset (laughs). At the same time if you are gay then there is no harassment of female employees. Gay men wouldn't be attracted to women thus leading to reduction in sexual harassment of women in the workplace.

If we assume the above narration to be true for all the gay men then we would be challenging the household model according to which gay men earn less than straight men, but if gay men have more time as they do not have as much relationship commitments and responsibility as compared to that of the heterosexual men then they should be earning more than the straight men provided that the culture and environment of the organisation is not homophobic, that they are working in an equal opportunity workplace and/or they are not visibly queer or out in their workplace. This may be true for some of the gay men but cannot be generalised, as not all the gay men have feminine attributes, not all the gay men can read male and female mind-set and such qualities vary from person to person, irrespective of their sexual orientation. With the above assumptions, the household model for lesbians earning more than heterosexual women would hold true not because all the lesbians have masculine attributes or are looked at with a masculine identity in all the organisations, institution and ultimately the society but because they would have more time as compared to that of the straight women due to major reasons, such as not all the lesbian women would have to choose between work and family unlike most Indian women. Lesbian women would have more time which could be spent on work. Further, for lesbian women the rate of getting married would be much lower compared to that of heterosexual women. Even lesbians would not have to go through the process of becoming a biological mother (like most married women in India) of a child and even if they decided to do it such a case would be very rare. All these things would give them more time which they can use to build their career. This would also hold true for gay men. Further, in a country like India the percentage of the population getting married (due to arrange marriage) is much higher as compared to that of the US and European nations. If Indian gay and lesbian individuals decided not to get married to the opposite gender because of societal pressure, then there would be a higher probability for them to be successful in their career as compared to that of the Indian men and women who get married; especially Indian women for whom most of the time marriage means a long break or end of their professional carrier. The household model can be challenged with quantitative research studies which should be conducted in future as the assumptions on which the household model is based can also not be generalised for all LGBTIQ populations all over the world who are a part of organisations and societies with a different culture and varied acceptance level.

Most of the individuals from the LGBTQ community thought that organisational culture and environment makes or breaks the deal for an employee belonging to the community. If the organisation is queer-friendly and treats people from the community no different than the heterosexual employees, then it would be possible for employees from the community to be accepted in the leadership and decision making roles. A participant, who is out in his organisation to some employees, shares his experience of difference in corporate culture in his previous organisation which had inclusive policies for the LGBTIQ community and his current Indian organisation where people would not tolerate even a discussion on such tabooed subjects.

> *See there are two leaders who are gay and respected in the organisation but both of them are closeted. So I cannot say that if they were open and gay would they still be leaders because they are closeted right now and they are at the topmost position of the organisation. For me, it might be a problem, but I guess again it would depend on the company that I am working with. At ABC (the previous organisation) I don't think such a thing should have happened. In fact, it would have probably taken me higher because it would reveal the fact that I have integrity, I am honest and that I have strong leadership quality because being out in open is a leadership quality. But in an Indian based company which is conservative, it may work as a disadvantage because they may think that if my subordinate finds out that I am gay then I won't be able to command enough of respect.* A gay participant

We could see that leadership by the members of the LGBTQ community at their workplace was mostly associated with the leader being autocratic. Further, if the leader had to be autocratic in nature it was perceived that the leader needed to be masculine so that they would be in a position to command/order their subordinates. The words used for associating leadership were very masculine as well. At times, it felt that some individuals, especially those who identified as gay and were not cis-gender, trans-gender or were visibly queer had convinced themselves that they would never be able to be in a leadership position or be respected when in a leadership position not only because they could not fulfil the expected norms of the way a leader is supposed to be but also because they thought that it would be very difficult for people to accept them as leaders as they would not be identified as an insider by most of their colleagues. So even when an individual from the community thought that they might be able to be autocratic to an extent and order other employees, it would be difficult for them to be respected by their colleagues and/or employees in the real sense.

Participants pointed out that a leader is seen as someone who is masculine, dependable and can take control of situations. People from the community, especially gay men or men having feminine characteristics are not considered masculine, dependable and rational enough to be a leader. It becomes essential for a leader to carry themselves in an "appropriate" manner. People would not want to be represented by a man who has effeminate attributes. It may not be difficult for a person who is closeted and acts in a gender appropriate manner, but for someone who challenges the very base of heteronormativity would have to deal with issues such as lack of trust and confidence with their subordinates and colleagues. Subordinates may continue to work under such a person, but would not respect the person, their sexual orientation and gender identity. During the interview, two participants said they know effeminate people in their organisation who were in the leadership position (irrespective of their sexual orientation) and not treated with respect due to this feminine attribute.

> *Forget sexual orientation, even with women employers they have a pre-concluded notion that women employees cannot reach the top. So when we look at the sexual minority community or particular sexual orientation of those particular communities, I think people mock you, make fun of it, do not take you seriously. I have seen that a friend of mine who has not come out but his behaviour is very pansy so people make fun of him. But he is at a (leadership) position that is a problem for him. Most of the people do not take him seriously.* A gay participant

All the transgenders felt that it would become difficult for employees to have a transgender person leading them. A transsexual man who has undergone surgery said:

> *People will never understand us, forget leadership. They think on a different tangent altogether.*

Only three participants felt that leadership qualities differ from person to person and that there is no relationship between gender identity and sexual orientation of the people with that of their acceptance and ability to lead. A participant who believed that leadership should not be a function of masculinity or heteronormativity said:

> *I think when you talk about leadership then you talk about functional capabilities. There are so many gay men who have feminine behaviour. I think leaders should be who they are and they should lead effectively. People should be judged on how you perform rather than your behaviour. This also implies to LGBT people. I judge them on the results.*

DOES DIVERSITY AND INCLUSION POLICY MATTERS?

The participants who worked in organisations which had inclusive and diversity policies felt that it was due to the legal, political and socio-cultural environment of our country (India) that the organisations could not think beyond discrimination. Organisations should have inclusive policies for the LGBT community, but such policies should not be inclusive only on paper. This inclusivity should also become part of the organisational culture.

Participants who were out in the organisation insisted that there was a need to have formal written inclusive policies which would embrace and enhance diversity at the workplace. Though all the participants thought that every organisation should have a formal written policy which gets translated in the work culture, some felt that even if the organisation does not have a written policy but embraces diversity and inclusion for the LGBTQ community, then they are moving in the right direction. Just having a policy or a one-liner in their larger policy does not ensure that the organisation will be an accepting and safe space for people from the community. With the given conditions that the people from the community face every day in India most of the people from the community will be happy if their organisation makes attempts to address discrimination for non-normative gender and sexual orientation identities within the workplace.

Various individuals from the community said that their organisation did not have a separate policy for the inclusion of employees from the community, but only a one-liner in the employee contract form which was handed to employees before joining the company. According to them, such statement(s) were inoperable because discrimination did take place as the organisation did not have a concrete system and redressal mechanism for handling issues related to sexual orientation and gender identity.

> *We need to understand that policy is not a word or a statement. The organisations need to define the policy so that it does not discriminate against sexuality. The policy should clearly communicate that the organisation does not allow gender and sexuality discrimination. A policy without education or sensitisation is as good as not having a policy at all. Every company shows you a presentation on what their company policy is...have you made an effort to define the terms such as homosexual, heterosexual, lesbian over there? Would you take a transgender person walking in your office and not look down upon that person? Would you have a Hijra person walking into your office...are you not going to have your eyes popping out? Are you going to let that person walk into your office as other people will walk into that office? You cannot have 'no discrimination' and then discrimination within that no discrimination, just because you did not define the term discrimination.* A gay participant

The anti-discriminatory policies are not well defined and are included in the human resource policy. So eventually, these policies form a very small part of the overall human resource policy of the company. No effort is taken to actually include the LGBT community. Even though the company may have a policy, they have not taken any effort to have a resource centre for educating employees and protecting the LGBT community. If at all there is a policy which is addressing gender discrimination and harassment, it is constructed keeping in mind that there are only two genders, man and woman, where man is the harasser and woman is the victim. Even if there are policies on discrimination, organisations assume, implement and practice heteronormativity. A participant said

> *See there is no LGBT policy. You have an anti-discriminatory policy and when we speak about an anti-discriminatory policy you just have a term which would be gender, sexuality and when you speak about gender, I do not think that people know that there is gender beyond male and female. So any time you speak about gender, you speak about sexuality in the larger context in India in many places it is more about not making loose comments on women. First of all, people do not understand that men could also be going through teasing or sexual harassment and they do not understand that there are sexualities and genders besides heterosexual (identities) and genders which are beyond male and female.*

While interacting with several individuals from the community, we understood that not only most of the organisations operating in India did not care about the rights of the LGBTQ individuals but also that diversity, in general, was not considered important by most of the organisations. Organisations did not value diversity in a country which is known for diversity. For most organisations, it seemed that the focus was just on profit maximisation at any cost. Further, any diversity initiative that organisations carry out is also driven by the motive of maximising profits as these activities would ultimately result either in the marketing of these organisations or would be implemented as a result of the law of the land. Most Indian organisations have diversity and inclusion policy at the workplace for women. One should not be surprised when they come to know that these diversity and inclusion policies exist because there are laws that protect the right of women in the workplace. For instance, when an organisation is providing sexual harassment training at the workplace, they may show it as being part of their diversity and inclusion policy, but all that these organisations are doing is trying their best to comply with the law of land. Further, most of the time diversity is understood as the just representation of a "minority" community in numbers, and there is hardly any practice to really make the culture inclusive for these individuals. For instance, acts of sexual harassment on women in the workplace are only seen as "defamation" of organisations goodwill and name. Majority of the organisations are not concerned about the impact of such incidences of sexual harassment on the victim. When women are not safe in the workplace despite policies and laws, it becomes even more difficult to think for safety and acceptance of the people from LGBTIQ community. We have seen the legal definition of sexual harassment and rape change in India, but are these definitions gender neutral and inclusive? Organisations should have gender-neutral policies to protect the rights of all gender and sexual orientation of any woman, man or a transgender. Though all the participants affirmed that their organisation had policies and mechanism for prevention, prohibition and redressal of sexual harassment of women in the workplace, they would refrain from taking legal action and these policies would remain on paper unless an "extreme" case had occurred. An attempt is made to settle instances of sexual harassment on women informally. A participant who worked for one of the biggest print media company in India said:

> My organisation tends to be a bit nervous about dealing with cases of sexual harassment on women...like most organisations, it follows cases in a very unstructured manner. There have been issues of harassment of women at my workplace. My organisation tries to solve these issues informally as much as possible. So simply, if you ask me that if my organisation follows guidelines of the Vishaka committee then probably not. In extreme case, it would follow the guidelines but otherwise, it would try to solve the issue in an informal way.

Employees of the organisation represent the organisation and convey the values of the organisation to the people they meet. It becomes necessary for the organisation to clear its stand on various issues. The organisations should have an ethical standard and all the employees of the organisation have to be aware of the same. The organisation should not leave room for assumptions to the employees of what the employees think of the organisational culture rather the organisations have to take a proactive step to first define its culture, values and ethical standards and then implement and educate/sensitise about the same to its employees. Even small steps taken by the organisation to make the LGBTIQ employees comfortable can play a significant role in boosting the morale of the employees. A participant who worked in an insurance company which did not have any formal inclusive and diversity policy felt contented when his organisation made "being queer-friendly" as one of the criteria for selection of the applicants. Since this organisation expected and recruited the applicants to be queer-friendly, the queer employees already working in the organisation also expected that the organisation would always protect their rights and provide them with a safe space even when they did not have a formal written policy.

> *In the training session, we give topics to employees to express their views…so that they can open up. I gave the topic of what they feel about LGBT people for instance if your brother or sister is gay then how will you react? That was the question which was taken by the AGM of the company in the list of 10 sets of questions which would be asked to the applicant during the interview to see if they were homophobic.*

There are very few organisations which have a written policy for the inclusion of the LGBTQ employees and also ensure that these policies are translated into actions. Further, organisations that have supported LGBTQ rights in India understand the law and have clarity on the journey/narrative that they want to be part of even when at times it means challenging the law of the land to lead the way for global LGBTQ rights.

References

Beauregard, T.A., et al. 2007. Revisiting the Social Construction of Family in the Context of Work. *Journal of Managerial Psychology* 24 (1): 46–65.

Concannon, L. 2008. Citizenship, Sexual Identity and Social Exclusion: Exploring Issues in British and American Social Policy. *International Journal of Sociology and Social Policy* 28 (9/10): 326–339.

Goodman, N.R. 2013. Taking Diversity and Inclusion Initiatives Global. *Industrial and Commercial Training* 45 (3): 180–183.

Myers, V. 2015, December 10. *Diversity Is Being Invited to the Party: Inclusion Is Being Asked to Dance.* https://www.youtube.com/watch?v=9gS2VPUkB3M. Accessed 15 January 2018.

CHAPTER 6

Conclusion

When we started the research, our primary objective was to capture the experiences and voices of LGBTQ individuals in the workplace in India. One of the primary objectives was to understand the impact of non-normative gender and sexual orientation identity of LGBTQ employees on their professional growth opportunities. While we started with the aim of knowing about the situation of the LGBTQ community in the workplace, we also understood a lot about our society and the possible reasons that a majority of the society not only chooses to turn a blind eye on the struggles of the LGBTQ but also creates additional problems for the individuals with non-normative identities. Considering that heterosexuality is a norm and is restricted in many parts of the country, one can logically understand why homosexuality is strictly forbidden.

Many people in India even today believe that individuals who identify with a queer or homosexual identity should either be punished or sent for corrective treatment. One should not be surprised if a person has even strong sentiments such as: all homosexuals should be given capital punishment by the government officials or killed by the civil society for engaging in sexual acts as it is considered immoral by the society. We also noticed that there was a lot of resentment and barriers that people had around these issues. Despite meeting people with such radical views on the LGBTQ community, we were able to interact with many individuals who were open and willing to have a difficult conversation. Having a conversation around issues which are not discussed is the first big step towards making a positive change in any society. What we understood while interacting with various people was that most of them had many questions related to sexuality, gender and the LGBTQ community, but there were not enough safe spaces and platforms where these discussions could freely be initiated. In the concluding chapter, we would not argue and give various reasons to the organisations or the readers with regard to why inclusion and diversity matter, as we assume that individuals who are reading this already believe that inclusion of all the communities and every individual matters. There have been studies that try to promote inclusion and diversity of the LGBTQ community to the organisations by telling them the benefits of such diversity initiatives which the organisations have not been able to see for a long time. Research is now being conducted which points out the economic loss that a country suffers due to discrimination and exclusion of the LGBTQ community. However, we will not give reasons as we believe that the economic contribution of any other reason for how a community benefits the society should not be a reason for deciding if a particular community is "eligible" to be included in the society. We believe that the human rights of any marginalised community or any individual should not be seen in relation to the price that nations have to pay as a result of exclusionary practices. Everything in life cannot and should not be associated with its cost-benefit.

Need to Start Somewhere

We were approached by some of the organisations operating in India to understand the limitation and scope of the diversity and inclusion policies for LGBTQ employees. We think that just reminiscing that something could be done with respect to LGBTQ diversity is a good place to start from, but then organisations see more reasons for not starting these initiatives. Often, these initiatives end up even before they begin. The reason given by most of these organisations for not taking up diversity and inclusion for the LGBTQ community is often that it is too risky given the acceptance by the overall society and that the majority of the Indian population would not be able to understand these issues. The reality is that these organisations fail to understand the law (even when the law now does not criminalise same-sex activity between consenting adults) and also judge the Indian population for what they can and cannot understand. Historically, people from civil societies, union bodies and organisations have helped their nation by forming better and stronger laws. We also noticed that most of the times these organisations fail to implement these diversity initiatives because their motive was never in line with actually doing anything for their employees. Most of the time, the organisations based in India think about carrying on these activities in India because they have been instructed to do so by their global head office. In fact, we now feel that multinational organisations of Indian origin which have their head offices in India are now being more sensitive about these issues as compared to global organisations operating in India having their headquarters in the US.

Often, our friends from NGOs and civil society criticise the corporates and organisations for turning a deaf ear towards the situation of the marginalised community. Some even blame these organisations and capitalism for worsening the situation and encashing on the pink money. It is often believed that most organisations based in India are conducting corporate social responsibility (CSR) activities because the law now mandates it and not because they want to contribute to society.

Considering the place where we come from and the conditions that we have seen of the LGBTQ community in India, we feel that any place is a good place to start from, but it is high time we started.

Initiating Difficult Conversations

Not only individuals who identified with the LGBTQ community but also heterosexuals felt safe and included in organisations which provided such spaces where difficult conversations could be initiated. Initiating conversations around sexuality and gender within these organisations made employees, people associated with the organisation and even civil society realise that these are the conversations that matter. A simple email by the leaders of the organisation to all its employees stating that they are there with their employees and that they believe in equal opportunity can go a long way in engaging and retaining employees. Further, this is not just applicable to LGBTQ diversity but any form of diversity and inclusion. Most of the time, all that the employees what to hear from their employers is that they are valued and their identities are respected. Further, organisations should create spaces where two-way communication can take place, and it is not just top-down communication at all times when it comes to addressing the diversity and inclusion initiatives. It is only when the leaders and managers in the organisations listen to their employees and involve them they will be able to understand what are the issues that bother most of them. However, even before the employers can listen to their employees, they need to create safe spaces and give time to their employees to open up.

Creating Safe Spaces and Giving Space to People

Often people ask us two questions when they come to know about this research. "Why this research?" and "How many people are from the LGBTQ community in India?" From our experience with people, the first question "Why this research?" can be interpreted in two ways. The first interpretation is that our identity is assumed to be that from the queer community and the second is that some of these people do not think that such research is adding any real value to the contribution of knowledge and/or do not have any real implications. Our interpretation of the second question "How many people are from the LGBTQ community in India?" is that most people think that since there are not enough people from the LGBTQ community who are visible in our society, the research does not matter. This is also one of the reasons that the Supreme Court of India has reinstated Section 377 of the IPC as the judges felt that since people from the community are a "minuscule minority," it does not matter if we have laws that affect their rights.

Before September 2018, most organisations would not do any diversity and inclusion initiatives because of Section 377 of the IPC which criminalised homosexuality. Now that same-sex activity between consulting adults is no more a crime, organisations are still not keen on having diversity and inclusion initiatives, and even when they have them, then these initiatives remain very superficial. Often, human resource and diversity managers have told us that there are not enough people or there is no one from the community in their organisation for them to think of these initiatives. Further, organisations which already have a policy for the inclusion of LGBTQ individuals often wonder about the reasons for not enough people coming out even when they have policies. In a democratic country like India, the rights of an individual or a community cannot be snatched away just because most people think that the representation of people from a particular community is very less. Even when there is none or when there are few individuals from the community, an organisation and society should not assume that the rights of this community do not matter just because they have minority status.

Coming out and disclosing the identity in a society where most of the spaces are heteronormative, and there are restrictions around discussion of identities that are considered non-normative is very difficult. Just because the organisation has a diversity and inclusion policy does not mean that an individual will come out, but this also does not mean that this should become an excuse for organisations for not having these initiatives and for not translating the already existing policy into praxis. Organisations need to not only create safe spaces for all individuals but also give space and time to individuals from the community to disclose their identity.

Everyone Is Valued

Individuals may not be out, but working in organisations which have policies that enable safe spaces gives a psychological relief and a strong sense of security to the employees. Further, we have interacted with employees who do not identify as queer but are proud to be working with an organisation which stands for LGBTQ rights as they might have a close association with individuals from the community outside their organisation. An individual whose younger brother is gay not only felt proud to be working in a place which values LGBTQ individuals but also felt that he could be more sensitive and exposed to the community, eventually resulting in strengthening the relationship with his brother due to sensitivity provided by his company. We also noted that many people who were aware of the LGBTQ issues thought that having LGBTQ diversity and inclusion in the workplace means that the employer embraces all forms and kinds of diversity and inclusion and values each individuals working in the organisation. This is because in India having LGBTQ diversity and inclusion initiatives is considered to be one of the most complex issues to address even by diversity and human resource experts. At the same time, the organisation which has diversity and inclusion for the LGBTQ community is seen to be very progressive and ahead of the times.

When It Is All About Productivity

During our interaction with heads, CEO's and CHRO's of various organisations in India, we had seen one common view among some of these professions that as long as people are productive it does not matter who they really are. These are leaders in an organisation who believe that the first and the most important thing that matters to them is that their employees are productive and which is also the most important criteria for career development and growth within the organisation. But what does productivity really means? If we have to simplify the definition of productivity for an organisation whose primary motive is to maximise profits, the definition would be output or contribution of/from a resource in relation to an existing standard. There is an intuitive assumption that the productivity of an employee who identifies as with LGBTQ community may be influenced negatively when discriminated. This may be assumed for any individual who is discriminated at their workplace and not just individuals from the LGBTQ community. In our research, we had seen that the overall wellbeing of an employee might be affected, but it is not necessary that it would lead to negative productivity. Productivity would depend on various factors such as the nature of the job; if individuals or a group perform the majority of the job, the power relations within the organisation, culture and value of the organisation, and the degree and nature of discrimination to name a few. We had noticed that at least in the short run even when an individual is facing verbal and/or non-verbal discrimination, it might be possible that there is no or minimal impact of these instances on the employee's productivity. A few participants have also reported that since they have a non-normative identity, they have always worked harder and learned new skills in a way to compensate for their identities. Some participants who were out or visibly queer also felt that they had got so used to listening to all the comments and that it had stopped affecting them. What we are trying to say is that discrimination or derogatory comments do definitely impact any individual in a negative way, but it may not always be reflected in their work productivity. In such cases, when an employer would only value productivity, then it would appear that everything is smoothly functioning in the organisation while failing to see the real problem.

In a case when the productivity of an individual is negatively affected, employers should understand that this might not only be because of the internal factors within the organisation but also be due to external factors in the society. For instance, an individual who identifies with the LGBTQ community, relationship with their family or unacceptance and discrimination from other spaces of the society may also affect the performance of the employee. If this employee is not out in the workplace, the employer will never understand the reasons due to which this individual is not able to perform well. Further, if the productivity of an individual may be affected due to internal factors such as discrimination at the workplace, the employer may not be able to reach the root of the problem due to lack of redressal mechanism, fear by the discriminated individual and lack of safe spaces. Ultimately, even when the productivity of an individual working in the organisation may be affected due to the internal or external factor or may not be affected at all, the employers and organisations should not just see human beings as an easily replaceable tool of production. An organisation which is just concerned about profits and not its people may not be able to sustain in the long run.

Having a Clear Stand

We have seen individuals from the community being confused as their organisations do not have a clear stand concerning diversity and inclusion of individuals from the LGBTQ community. Many individuals spend an extended period testing the waters in their organisation and understanding if their organisation would be accepting individuals with gender and sexual orientation identities that are considered non-normative. "Don't tell, Don't ask" is the norm in most of the organisations. Even when organisations are anti-LGBTQ rights, they should state it out loud. It would help people belonging to the community, irrespective of their closet status while choosing their potential employers or projects.

There have been instances when people in the leadership position of organisations have issued derogatory comments or shown bias towards the community openly due to which their business has also extensively suffered. Today in the era of globalisation when an organisation is directly or indirectly endorsing anti-LGBTQ statements, then they are aware or are being made aware by the global civil society that there is a vast possibility that they would be losing out on business and also customers who value LGBTQ rights. Today for organisations to come out and state clearly that they are anti-LGBTQ is becoming more difficult as more countries embrace equal rights for the LGBTQ community.

There are many organisations which state that they are equal employment opportunity providers, but fail to overcome bias and lack sensitivity towards the community. In India, one should not be surprised if the organisations that claim to be equal opportunity employers also end up discriminating people from the LGBTQ community not only during the recruitment process but also when an individual has been appointed. The COO of a multinational organisation, which is also an equal opportunity provider on paper, working in India, refused to greet and shake hands with a transsexual woman during the interview process. Further, organisations which have inclusion and diversity for the LGBTQ employees do not make an effort to explain or sensitise their employees about these policies. The policy for LGBTQ employees forms a very small part of the entire policy for the organisation—most of the time just a one-liner which also tells us the importance of these initiatives and policies in the organisation.

It is difficult to get things right at the first time especially when we are thinking of safe spaces and diversity and inclusion for a community which has been neglected historically. Even if we do not get it right the first time, it is essential that we try. It is vital for individuals and organisations to be mindful and reflexive for continuous and inclusive growth. Often managers say that LGBT diversity is very complicated to understand, but if we understand what diversity and inclusion for any individual or community is, we would not have an issue with understanding LGBTQ diversity. Broadly there is not much of a difference between diversity for LGBTQ individuals in comparison to any other form of diversity. If the organisation aims to design an environment that is universally accessible by all, then they would not find much difficulty in understanding an LGBTQ diversity and inclusion initiative which is often considered complex. Most Indian organisations do not think about diversity other than diversity for women. Further, most of these diversity and inclusion policies are activities and infrastructure that has been mandated by the law. It was interesting for us to see that some organisations have now also started thinking about generational diversity. This could be possible because the older employees in the top and middle management are feeling redundant with changes in competencies required for effectively performing in the corporate world. It is sad to say, but we have learned during the course of research that the top management of most organisations would only initiate diversity actions either when it is a mandate by law or when the top management might themselves be affected. For most organisations, diversity still means hiring a certain quota, providing reservations or percentage of people in the organisation. We hope that more organisations in future would truly create tangible and intangible structures which facilitate diversity and inclusion as a value and not just a mandate or number!

Glossary

Reference for the glossary: www.dictionary.com

Note by the authors: During our interaction with various people, we realised that not many people in India are aware about the queer identities and LGBTQ terminologies. Often, there is confusion with respect to how an identity is defined. Further, we also wanted to share our interpretation for a few terms/words especially in the context of this book. In this glossary, we have provided a list of words with a brief definition that are frequently used in this book. Although most of these definitions are taken from the online open source website www.dictionary.com, we have added/modified some of these definitions so that it is easier for us to convey our message as well as for the readers to understand the usage of these words in this book. The readers should note that these words may be defined/interpreted differently, depending on the individual, situations and/or context.

Agender A person who does not identify with a specific gender expression.

Ally An individual who supports the LGBTQ community, but does not identify with any queer identity.

Androgyne Person appearing and/or identifying as neither man nor woman, presenting a gender either mixed or neutral.

Asexual An individual who is not sexually attracted to anyone or does not have a sexual orientation, however, may be emotionally or romantically attracted to another person.

Bi-curious Curious about or open to exploring sexual relations with those from different gender.

Bisexual A person romantically, sexually or physically to men and women, or to people of various gender identities; ambisexual.

Butch In this research, "Butch" is used to signify physically masculine women or lesbians. It is sometimes used as a derogatory term for lesbians, but it can also be claimed as an affirmative identity label. The broader definition of butch would be a person who identifies themselves as masculine, whether physically, mentally or emotionally.

Cis-gender Related to a person whose gender identity corresponds with that person's biological sex assigned at birth.

Coming Out The process/action of disclosure/acknowledgement of an individual's non-normative gender and/or sexual orientation identity.

Cross-Dresser To dress in clothing's typically worn by members of the opposite sex. Most of the time, cross-dressing is with the intention of performing a different gender role/identity.

Discrimination For this research, discrimination is defined as biased or prejudicial treatment of individuals due to their sexual orientation, gender identity and/or performativity of gender, resulting in a denial of opportunity or unfair treatment.

Fag Derogatory/offensive term referring to an individual's homosexuality.

FTM/F2M Abbreviation for female-to-male transgender or a transsexual person who is in the process of transition or now has masculine gender identity.

Gay Relating to, or exhibiting sexual, romantic and emotional desire or behaviour directed towards a person or person's own sex, in most cases referring to a man attracted to other men.

Gender Binary A classification system consisting of two genders, male and female (also referred to as traditional gender model in this book).

Gender Identity A person's inner sense of identifying/belonging with a/more gender identity.

Gender Normative An individual who confirms with the "normative" gender identity (in most societies, heterosexuality is the norm and homosexuality or the queer identity becomes non-normative gender identity).

Gender Oppression Exercise of authority or power in a burdensome, cruel or unjust manner due to one's gender identity.

Gender Variant Relating to a person whose gender identity or gender expression does not conform to socially defined gendered norms.

Genderqueer or Queer An individual having a gender identity that is other than male or female, is a combination of the two genders, or is on a continuum between different genders. It may also mean someone who is questioning either his or her gender identity or the gender binary. In the past (and at times even today), the word queer had been used as a derogatory term to refer to an individual who does not identify or performs gender as per the heteronormative binary. However, the word has been reclaimed and is now commonly used as a gender identity.

Heteronormativity When heterosexuality becomes the norm in society.

Heterosexism A prejudiced attitude or discriminatory practices against homosexuals by heterosexuals.

Homosexual An individual sexually, romantically and/or emotionally attracted to another person from the same gender.

In the Closet Refers to hiding/not disclosing one's non-normative gender and/or sexual orientation identity.

Intersexed Person An individual having reproductive organs or external sexual characteristics of a different biological gender, mostly male and female.

Lesbian Relating to a woman exhibiting sexual, romantic and emotional desire or behaviour directed towards another woman. Sometimes individuals who identify as lesbian may also refer themselves as gay.

LGBTIQ Abbreviation for the lesbian, gay, bisexual, transgender, intersexed and queer community.

MTF/M2F Abbreviation for male-to-female transgender or transsexual person who is in the process of transition or now has feminine gender identity.

Outing For our research, outing refers to the act of disclosing/revealing another individual's sexual orientation and/or gender identity without obtaining consent from these individuals.

Pansexual Also omnisexual. Expressing or involving sexuality in all its forms, or sexual activity with individuals from any sexual orientation or gender identity. Also used by bisexual individuals at times as a more politically correct term, which does not divide gender into binary.

Passing The ability of an individual to come across with gender normative behaviour/identity even when they may not identify with these identities.

Polyamory The practice or condition of participating simultaneously in more than one romantic or sexual relationship with the knowledge and consent of all partners.

Sex Here referring to biological sex; it is the identification of individuals with respect to their reproductive function.

Sexual Orientation One's preference in sexual partner.

Sexual Reassignment Surgery (SRS) When an individual undergoes a medical surgery to attain a gender identity or expression that they might not have been their biological sex at birth.

Straight An individual who identifies as heterosexual.

Straight-Acting A queer/homosexual individual who passes or performs gender to pass as a heterosexual individual.

Trans*/Transgender An umbrella term that individuals use when their gender identity does not correspond to their biological sex assigned at birth.

Transition The process or period that individuals go through while attaining/performing the desired gender identity/expression.

Transvestite Refer to cross-dresser above.

After going through this glossary, if you feel that you would want to further know in detail about the LGBTQ terminology, definitions and gender-neutral pronouns, then we would suggest you to visit the website (link: https://www.lgbt.ucla.edu/Resources/LGBTQ-Terminology) by UCLA Lesbian Gay Bisexual Transgender Campus Resource Center.

Index[1]

A
Abnormal, 22, 52, 65, 108
Accepting, 20, 26, 28, 30, 45, 61, 66, 111–117, 123, 133
Affirmative actions, 14
AIDS, 14
Androgynous, 6
Anti-discrimination law, 1
Appearance, 8, 10, 25, 75
Assumptions, 10, 11, 22, 29, 34, 49, 63, 64, 71, 95, 120, 125, 131
Authentic gender model, 6–12
  Samuel Lurie, 6
Awareness, 2, 4, 15, 60, 83, 87

B
Background check, 96, 97
Bias, 4–7, 21, 35, 50, 64, 106, 133
Biological sex, 4, 6, 8, 22, 34, 41, 71
Body language, 9, 35, 71–75
Budget, 102
Butch, 26, 69, 72, 74, 113

C
Capitalism, 3, 14–16, 129
Capital punishment, 127
Career, 11n1, 23, 25, 30, 44, 48, 49, 53, 56, 58, 84, 113, 117–120, 131
Carnal intercourse, 18, 19, 108
Caste system, 14–16
Change, v, vi, 2, 3, 5, 9, 10, 13, 16, 21, 39, 43, 55, 58, 67, 75, 78, 101, 102, 116, 117, 125, 128, 134
Cis-gender, 17, 34, 37–39, 51, 57, 58, 68, 72, 109, 121
Closet, 3, 20, 28, 45–47, 52, 53, 57, 58, 63, 65, 133
Co-habitants, 82, 83
Coming out, 5, 20, 23, 24, 28, 43–53, 55, 56, 61, 65, 88–93, 110, 130
Community, v, 1, 21–30, 34, 63, 81, 105, 127
Compensation, 23–25, 28, 105
Compensations schemes, 105
Compliance, 29, 50
Concealment strategy, 68

[1] Note: Page numbers followed by 'n' refer to notes.

© The Author(s) 2020
S. Palo, K. K. Jha, *Queer at Work*,
https://doi.org/10.1007/978-981-13-8562-9

Conditioning, 5–6
Confronting, 57
Consensual, 3, 12, 13, 20, 107, 110
  consenting, 20
Conversations, vii, 4, 10, 21, 24, 35, 45, 48, 54, 59, 60, 64, 82, 91, 95, 102, 103, 127, 129
Coping mechanism, 33–62
Corrective measures, 5, 61, 65, 72
Couple, 7–10, 18, 37, 69, 71, 92, 95, 105, 106, 108, 109
Courtesy stigma, 28, 56–57
Criminalisation, 8, 17
  criminalised, 3, 14, 20, 130
Cultural segregation, 68

D

Deconstruction, 10
Decriminalisation, 3, 20, 21
Delhi, 17, 19, 20
Democratic, 109, 130
Depression, 38, 39, 43, 76
Derogatory remarks, 37–39, 42, 57, 71–73, 79, 114, 115
Deviance, 8–10
Difficult conversation, vii, 4, 21, 64, 102, 127, 129
Disagreement, 16
Disclosure, 8, 45, 47, 49, 51, 55, 90
  disclose, 7, 36, 44, 49, 50, 66, 78, 97, 106, 115, 118, 131
Discrimination
  differential treatment, 105
  non-verbal, 34–38, 40, 132
  physical, 35, 40–43, 99
  sexual harassment, 25, 40–43
  verbal, 35–40, 99
Discriminator, 16, 41
District Screening Committees, 13
Diversity, v, 4, 6, 21, 22, 28, 29, 35–37, 40, 48, 50, 52–54, 66,
88, 98, 102, 103, 105–108, 110, 111, 116, 122–126, 128–131, 133, 134
Dress code, 75–79
  formal, 78

E

Economic loss, 128
Education, 4, 14, 123
Effeminate, 26, 40, 74, 99, 112, 113, 121, 122
Employment, 14, 21, 43, 44, 58, 76, 77, 83, 96, 97, 106, 117
Equal employment opportunity, 44, 133
Equal rights, 16, 17, 22, 24, 28, 60, 99, 108, 133
Existence, 3, 11, 18, 28, 60, 66
Exploitation, 109
Extended family, 60, 61
External environment, 92, 102
Extorted, 19

F

Fear, 12, 14, 19, 20, 23, 24, 28, 41, 43–46, 48, 50, 55–57, 59, 61, 67, 83, 84, 88, 100, 118, 132
Female to male (F2M), 5, 24
Feminine, 5, 6, 19, 26, 38, 42, 66, 71–74, 76, 79, 94, 113, 114, 117, 119–122
Flow of information, 28, 48, 53, 68, 100–102
Fluid, 8, 9, 109

G

Gender appropriate dressing, 75–80
Gender binary, 6, 8, 28, 78
Gender imbalance, 25
Gender performance, 8, 74, 75

The gender quiz, 6, 8
Generational differences, 93
Gestational neuro-hormonal theory, 64, 65
Government, 12, 34, 48, 127

H
Harassment, 6, 19, 21, 22, 25, 26, 98, 105, 111, 113, 115, 119, 124, 125
Hate crime, 1, 16, 22, 64, 91
Healthcare, 14
Hegemonic discourse, 22, 34
Heteronormative, vi, 9, 18, 22, 28, 34, 43, 45, 50, 54, 59, 63–66, 71–74, 78, 80, 87, 101, 118, 130
  heteronormativity, 9, 11, 41, 55, 63–80, 106, 122, 124
Heterosexual, 4, 6, 7, 9–11, 18, 23, 24, 26, 28, 29, 37–39, 42, 50, 51, 54, 55, 57, 59, 63, 66–69, 71–73, 94, 102, 105, 108, 109, 116, 119, 120, 123, 124, 129
Hierarchy
  gender hierarchy, 25
  organisational hierarchy, 25
High Court, 3, 19–21, 46
Hijra, 11–14, 11n1, 11n2, 12n3, 12n4, 33, 87, 88, 123
  gharana, 12, 12n3, 12n4, 88
History of Sexuality, 3
HIV, 14
Homosexual, 9, 19, 21, 22, 26, 34, 45, 55, 60, 63–65, 67, 70, 94, 106, 109, 123, 127
Hostile attitude, 22, 108
Household specialisation model, 23–25
Human rights, v, 4, 5, 12, 14, 15, 17, 19, 20, 22, 60, 82, 105, 108, 128
Hyderabad, 2, 17, 36, 47, 70, 98, 99

I
Identifying, 11, 11n1, 14, 18, 19, 23, 27, 29, 34, 47, 49, 60, 63, 65, 84, 86, 87, 105, 109, 110
Identity, v, 2, 33–63, 81, 86–95, 106, 127
Identity crises, 33–62, 66
Ideologies, 14, 15, 17, 26, 60, 64
Illegal, 21, 94, 110
Implicit inversion theory, 23
Inclusion, v, 6, 21, 28, 29, 35–37, 40, 50, 52–54, 60, 66, 98, 102, 103, 105–108, 110, 111, 122–126, 128–131, 133, 134
India, v, 1, 36, 66, 82, 105, 127
Indian Penal Code (IPC), 3, 7, 12, 13, 17–21, 29, 41, 46, 99, 102, 108, 130
Indifferent behaviour, 1, 57
  indifferent attitude, 34–36
Industries, 27, 28, 72, 76, 82, 111–117
Inferior, 22, 108
Information technology, 61, 81–103
Intercourse, 18, 108, 109
Internet, 62, 81–103
  internet-enabled platforms, 93, 94, 97
Interpretation, 14, 19, 29, 49, 109, 130
Intersectionality, vii, 15–17, 22, 110
Intersex, vii, 2, 6, 14, 87
Invisible, 22, 24, 34
IPC, *see* Indian Penal Code
Isolation, 35, 45, 46, 118

J
Job satisfaction, 30
Judgement, 12, 13, 19, 20, 86, 91, 96, 99, 102, 118

K
Kissing, 8, 9

L

Labelling, 9, 110
Late technology adopters, 94
Leadership, 25, 29, 44, 106, 108, 110, 114, 117–122, 133
Legitimised, 21

M

Male to female (M2F), 24
Management, 26, 28, 29, 51, 67, 75, 112, 117, 119, 134
Marriage
  married, 9, 23, 24, 42, 50, 66–71, 94, 105, 119, 120
  unmarried, 37, 66, 67, 70
Masculinity
  inclusive, 25–27
  orthodox, 25, 26
Media, 47, 61, 78, 81–85, 90–92, 95–97, 99, 100, 111, 112, 114, 115, 125
Metropolitan city, 2, 60, 82–84, 87, 88
Mindful, 5, 9–11, 35, 134
Molested, 19, 41
Mumbai, 2, 15, 17, 38, 47, 70
Myths, 64

N

NALSA, 2, 3, 12–17, 19, 21, 29, 36, 47, 77, 78
Nature, vi, 5, 18, 19, 21, 22, 42, 47, 51, 54, 55, 60, 64, 72, 81, 95, 108, 109, 112, 121, 132
Network groups, 28
NGO, 89, 129
Non-disclosure, 45–47, 55, 89, 90
Non-normative, vi, 1, 2, 4, 5, 8, 18, 19, 21, 23, 24, 35, 36, 43–52, 54, 55, 57–59, 62, 64, 66–69, 71, 79, 81, 86–88, 90, 92, 93, 95–98, 100, 103, 106, 110, 112, 115, 118, 119, 123, 127, 130, 132, 133
Norm, 6, 9, 18, 25, 28, 38, 63, 64, 66, 69, 72, 75, 80, 90, 121, 127, 133
Normalising, 51, 52, 64, 70
Normative, vi, 4, 7, 8, 10, 11, 15, 17, 18, 21, 23, 41, 51, 54, 59, 66, 69, 72, 74, 75, 77, 95, 109
Nurtured, 64, 65

O

Occupational pensions, 105
Opportunity, vi, 6, 12, 26, 28, 34, 36, 43, 44, 50, 54, 57, 58, 76, 77, 83–85, 89, 91, 96, 99, 100, 102, 107, 114, 117, 119, 127, 129, 133
Oppression, 14–16, 91
Order of nature, 18, 19, 21, 108, 109
Organisation, 6, 34, 66, 85, 105–126, 128
Organisational climate, 49
Other, 15, 16, 33–62, 111–117

P

Participants, 6–10, 34, 37, 40, 43–46, 48, 53, 54, 57, 67–70, 72–75, 78, 79, 82, 83, 85, 86, 88, 89, 91, 92, 96, 98, 105–107, 111–125, 132
Partner, 7, 10, 17, 24, 50, 54, 55, 67, 69–71, 84, 94, 95, 106
Passing strategy, 70, 71, 100, 101
Patriarchy, 4, 14–17, 29
Penetration, 19
Peno-vaginal, 18, 55
  penile-vaginal, 19, 108, 109
Performativity, 34, 63, 108

Physical assault, 35, 41, 73
Picture, 7–10, 79, 96, 98, 99, 113
Policemen, 13, 19
Policy, 21, 22, 28–30, 35, 40, 48, 53, 59, 60, 75, 76, 78, 79, 96, 98, 105–108, 110, 111, 116, 121–126, 128, 130, 131, 133, 134
Prejudicial treatment, 33
Pressure, 9, 11, 24, 68, 120
Pride, 15, 17, 47, 48, 54, 87, 91, 98–100
Proactive, 29, 51, 125
Productivity, 35, 110, 131–132
Professor, 20, 21, 56
Protection, 14, 16, 41
Protection of Rights, 13, 14
Pseudo identity, 92, 93, 98

Q
Queer, 1–3, 6, 14, 15, 17, 19, 21, 25, 29, 34, 36, 37, 42, 44–47, 50, 55, 57, 59–63, 67–69, 71, 73, 75, 81–103, 105, 106, 108, 109, 111–115, 118, 120, 121, 126, 127, 130–132

R
Rape, 26, 41, 72, 109, 125
Real, 13, 24, 46, 61, 67, 81–103, 121, 130, 132
Recriminalisation, 3
Reflections, 2
Reflective, 11
Relationship, 7–10, 18, 19, 21, 23, 24, 26, 38, 51, 53–55, 57, 59, 62, 67–71, 84, 88, 93–95, 118, 119, 122, 131, 132
Religion, 17
Revocation, 17, 19, 96

S
Safe spaces, 2, 17, 45, 88, 101–103, 106, 108, 110, 123, 126, 128–133
Secondary, 16
Section 377, 3, 7, 12, 13, 17–21, 23, 24, 26, 29, 41, 46, 99, 102, 107–110, 130
Self-identified, 5, 9, 46, 73
Self-identifying, 4
Self-perceived image, 22, 34
Sensitisation, 9, 10, 123
Sex, 3, 4, 6, 8, 13, 14, 18, 20, 22, 34, 38, 41, 49, 62, 63, 65, 67, 70, 71, 74, 76, 82, 94, 108, 109
Sex reassignment surgery (SRS), 13, 21, 24, 62, 71, 89
Sexually transmitted disease (STD), 24
Signalling, 47, 51, 52
Social media
  digital footprints, 90
  social media footprints, 81
Social security, 105
Spillover effect, 48, 50, 53, 114
Stereotype, 4, 6, 7, 11, 18, 25–27, 57, 108, 110–113
Stigma, 5, 12, 13, 22, 24, 26, 48, 56, 61, 67, 68, 70, 89, 100, 101, 114
Stigma management, 67, 102
Stigmatising attitudes, 1
Sting operation, 81
Straight, 9, 10, 22–25, 34, 55, 59, 63, 65, 73–75, 107, 113, 119, 120
Strategies, 49–52, 55, 70, 71, 91, 96
Structural suppression, 48
Support system, 28, 39, 47, 52, 60, 61, 92
Supreme Court, 3, 12, 13, 20, 21, 46, 96, 99, 102, 107, 109, 130
Symbolic representation, 15

T

Taboo, 4, 65, 69
Tax collector, 12
tax defaulter, 12
Technology, 46, 81–85,
  88, 89, 91, 93–96,
  98, 101, 102
Third gender, 3, 12, 13, 19,
  27, 47, 78
Trade union, 28
Traditional gender model, 4–8, 11,
  13, 18, 28, 34, 52, 60
Traditional understanding of gender,
  4–5
Training, 6, 9, 10, 64, 124, 126
Truth, 46, 93, 111, 113

U

Unacceptable, 18
Un-gendering, 11
Unique, 6, 35
University, 20, 21
Unlearning, 11
Unnatural offences, 18, 108

V

Virtual
  groups, 60
  identity, 82, 92, 95, 100, 101, 103
  world, 92, 93, 95, 96, 101
Visibility, 28, 82, 85, 97, 108, 114, 116
Visibly queer, 34, 36, 37, 57, 63,
  67–69, 71, 73, 106, 114, 115,
  120, 121, 132

W

Workplace, v, vi, 1, 17, 20–30, 33, 34,
  37–40, 42–45, 48–55, 57–59,
  61–81, 85, 89, 97–103, 105,
  106, 110, 111, 115, 117–121,
  123–125, 127, 131, 132
Workplace culture, 66
Written policy, 106, 107, 123, 126

GPSR Compliance

The European Union's (EU) General Product Safety Regulation (GPSR) is a set of rules that requires consumer products to be safe and our obligations to ensure this.

If you have any concerns about our products, you can contact us on

ProductSafety@springernature.com

In case Publisher is established outside the EU, the EU authorized representative is:

Springer Nature Customer Service Center GmbH
Europaplatz 3
69115 Heidelberg, Germany

www.ingramcontent.com/pod-product-compliance
Lightning Source LLC
LaVergne TN
LVHW011007250326
834688LV00004B/109